T0182693

The POETRY of GRIEF, GRATITUDE, and REVERENCE

Edited by JOHN BREHM

Wisdom

Wisdom Publications
132 Perry Street
New York, NY 10014 USA
wisdomexperience.org

Library of Congress Cataloging-in-Publication Data
Names: Brehm, John, 1955– editor.
Title: The poetry of grief, gratitude, and reverence / edited John Brehm.
Description: New York: Wisdom Publications, 2024.
Identifiers: LCCN 2024005609 (print) | LCCN 2024005610 (ebook) |
    ISBN 9781614298724 (paperback) | ISBN 9781614298816 (ebook)
Subjects: LCSH: Grief—Poetry.
Classification: LCC PN6110.G85 P64 2024 (print) |
    LCC PN6110.G85 (ebook) | DDC 808.81—dc23/eng/20240206
LC record available at https://lccn.loc.gov/2024005609
LC ebook record available at https://lccn.loc.gov/2024005610

ISBN 978-1-61429-872-4   ebook ISBN 978-1-61429-881-6

28 27 26 25 24   5 4 3 2 1

Cover painting, *The Young Owl*, by Kevin Sloan.
Cover design by James Zaccaria.
Interior design by Tim Holtz. Set in Mrs Eaves 11.5/16.

Wisdom Publications' books are printed on acid-free paper and meet the
guidelines for permanence and durability of the Production Guidelines for
Book Longevity of the Council on Library Resources.

Printed in the United States of America.

Please visit fscus.org.

Contents

II. Gratitude

III. Reverence

Introduction

Poetry is a profoundly relational art, an invitation to connect: with the poet, with the poem, and through the poem with each other, with the deepest aspects of our shared human experience. Poetry is also, I believe, a fundamentally spiritual art. It draws on the same powers of insight and imagination, wisdom and compassion, wonder and awe that form the basis of our spiritual response to the world. Artistic expressions of that response extend as far back as the earliest cave art forty thousand years ago, where luminous half-human/half-animal beings seem to rise out of the rock from the spirit world. Some anthropologists now believe that such art was created by shamans and that the caves themselves were spaces where sacred rituals were performed. They have found that the paintings always appear in those caves with the greatest acoustic resonance and were thus best suited for singing. Right from the very beginning, the impulse to make art has been inseparable from a desire to make contact with the sacred.

In "O Darkness," which appears in the "Reverence" section of this anthology, Danusha Laméris points to the primal mystery at the heart of artistic-spiritual expression: "What we do not know lies in darkness. / The way the unsayable rests at the back of the tongue. / So let us sing of it. . ." What can't be said can be sung. And like song, poetry can become a conduit for the unsayable, a way to embody what lies just beyond our conscious knowing. My teacher A. R. Ammons put it this way: "Poetry is a verbal means to a non-verbal source . . . a motion to no-motion, to the still point of contemplation and deep realization." Not all poems take us to that still point or make contact with the sacred, but great poems do, and poetry itself—who knows how?—is inherently possessed of this power.

Within this broad framework of poetry as a fundamentally relational and spiritual art, I have chosen to organize this collection around the themes of grief, gratitude, and reverence for several reasons: because these emotions can move us beyond the small self and its egoic concerns; because they call us to remember our true nature, who we really are; and because they offer the felt experience of connection we all long for, consciously or unconsciously. But those reasons did not fully emerge until well after I had started thinking about this book. In truth, I felt drawn to the themes grief, gratitude, and reverence without at first exactly knowing why.

In December of 2021, while I was staying on the Oregon coast, the shape of this collection finally came into focus. I had been wanting to create another anthology, one devoted exclusively to modern and contemporary poetry, ever since *The Poetry of Impermanence, Mindfulness, and Joy* was published in 2017. But it wasn't until that winter day, sitting on a rock looking out at the Pacific, that the three themes of the anthology suddenly came to me. I felt some initial resistance—I was uncertain about how grief, gratitude, and reverence fit with each other—but they kept suggesting themselves to me, and in the end it felt right to bring them together even if I didn't fully understand how they were connected. I trusted that a deeper underlying logic would make itself clear. I knew at the outset that they represented powerful emotional states we needed to experience, individually and collectively, in a much more conscious and embodied way.

~

Our world is awash in unprocessed grief, a heavy burden we most often try to bear alone and in silence, or to push away altogether. In *The Wild Edge of Sorrow: Rituals of Renewal and the Sacred Work of Grief*, Francis Weller suggests that "our refusal to welcome the sorrows that come to us, our inability to move through these experiences with true presence and conscious awareness, condemns us to a life shadowed by grief." But he also shows that when we turn and face our grief, we come more fully alive. "It is the broken heart, the part that knows sorrow, that is capable of genuine love." The poems I've gathered in the "Grief" section arise from such a turning toward, from a sustained and conscious engagement with loss and grief.

And if it is the broken heart that is capable of genuine love, it also the broken heart that is capable of the most profound gratitude. We can't fully appreciate the preciousness of life until we feel its fragility, its impermanence, until we have known loss. Moving into the poetry of gratitude after the poetry of grief mirrors an organic progression in our emotional lives. Loss can open a path to gratitude and connection, even as the journey there may be beset by loneliness, bitterness, and despair. And just as turning toward grief can be liberating, cultivating a grateful orientation toward life, rather than simply feeling grateful when good things come our way and resentful when they don't, can engender a fundamental shift in the way we move through the world: from resistance and judgment to acceptance and a profound, ongoing appreciation for life's moment-by-moment unfolding. The poems in the "Gratitude" section embody and exemplify this shift.

The conscious experience of a gratitude born of grief can take us all the way to reverence. *Reverence* is a word one rarely encounters these days. Indeed, one of the few recent books devoted to the subject,

Reverence by Paul Woodruff, bears the subtitle *Renewing a Forgotten Virtue*. But if reverence is indeed a largely forgotten virtue (my Christian friends tell me otherwise), it is still deeply embedded in our psyches, part of our ancient human lineage, our spiritual DNA. And perhaps it would be more true to say that reverence, which derives from the Latin *reverentia*, literally "to stand in awe of," has not been forgotten so much as banished, since it is incompatible with the foundational assumptions of our increasingly technological culture: the reductive, mechanistic, radically materialist worldview that is so thoroughly interwoven into all aspects of our lives we're hardly aware of it. In an economic system predicated on unlimited growth and ever-increasing profits, reverence for the earth and for our non-human brothers and sisters becomes an impediment, a feeling that must be suppressed for full-scale exploitation and resource extraction to continue. Like many others, I have come to believe that recovering a sense of reverence, a sense of the sacredness of all life, may be the only thing that can save us from the total systems collapse that now looms before us, if indeed it is not already too late. Writer, farmer, and ecological activist Wendell Berry has argued eloquently that "it is only on the condition of humility and reverence before the world that our species will be able to remain in it." The stakes are that high.

My belief is that poetry has a vital role to play in the collective awakening that must happen if we are to survive and flourish.

We are all subject to the law of impermanence, our lives inevitably marked and often dramatically altered by loss and grief. No one is exempt. But grief, as painful and private as it often feels, has the potential to create the deepest human bonds. Ada Limón's "Downhearted," which begins this anthology, speaks directly to our need to share the burden of grief:

Six horses died in a tractor-trailer fire.
There. That's the hard part. I wanted
to tell you straight away so we could
grieve together.

Even an indirect experience of tragedy, reading about the kind of horror Limón points to, can feel overwhelming, can make us want to withdraw from the world, pull our hand back from the flame, close our hearts. But if we can grieve together, we may find a way to be with the pain. We may come to see that grief does not have to isolate us but can instead connect us with a universal experience.

The parable of the mustard seed from the Buddhist scriptures illuminates this inexorable aspect of the human predicament. As the story goes, one day the Buddha was approached by Kisa, a young mother crazed with grief over the death of her infant son, her only child. Unable to accept the loss, she carried her child to the Buddha and implored him to bring her son back to life. The Buddha heard her pleas with compassion and said that he could create a medicine that would restore her son but that to do so he would need a mustard seed, which he instructed her to find in a nearby village. This mustard seed, however, had to come from a home that had never been touched by death. Kisa went from door to door asking for such a seed. All the villagers were willing to help, but none lived in a house that had not experienced a death. Finally, Kisa realized that the pain of loss was not hers alone but universal and inescapable, a burden shared by all. With that realization she became a follower of the Buddha and entered the path of liberation.

Joy Harjo's "Speaking Tree" explores how this sense of aloneness after great loss intensifies our grief. She begins by naming some of the things that are "unspeakable" on the earth: "A shy wind threading leaves after a massacre," the "cries of anguish" of trees "when they are broken and bereft." And then she gives voice to a piercing vulnerability, her own cry of anguish: "I carry a yearning I cannot bear alone in the dark. / What shall I do with all this heartache?" Here, it isn't so much the yearning that can't be borne but the aloneness, having no place to put the pain, no one to hold the heartache with her. But in writing the poem, she does make a space for her suffering, a space that can be shared, with us. And when we enter the poem with an open heart, not only do we help the poet carry her sorrow but the poem in turn helps us carry our own.

Poet and critic Edward Hirsch writes that elegy "ritualizes grief into language and thereby makes it more bearable. The great elegy touches the unfathomable and originates in the unspeakable, in unacceptable loss. . . . It drives a wordless anguish, wordless torment, toward the consolations of verbal articulation, verbal ceremony." In the act of reading such a poem, we participate in that ceremony and complete the arc from unspeakable suffering to the healing power of communion.

Human beings are hardwired to connect, not just with each other but with the earth itself and all its manifestations of life, as so many of the poems in this anthology attest. Rilke knew this truth, a truth we have been taught to forget, and expresses it beautifully in this sonnet to Orpheus:

> See the flowers, so faithful to Earth.
> We know their fate because we share it.
> Were they to grieve for their wilting,
> that grief would be ours to feel.

There's a lightness in things. Only we move forever
    burdened,
pressing ourselves into everything, obsessed by
    weight.
How strange and devouring our ways must seem
to those for whom life is enough.

If you could enter their dreaming and dream with
    them deeply,
you would come back different to a different day,
moving so easily from that common depth.

Or maybe just stay there: they would bloom and
    welcome you,
all those brothers and sisters tossing in the meadows,
and you would be one of them.

The kinship Rilke invites us to imagine, seeing the
flowers as our "brothers and sisters," is one that
our hunter-gatherer ancestors knew intimately for
millions of years. That sense of kinship hasn't van-
ished; it has simply been vitiated by an economic

system that runs on grasping and aversion. "How strange and devouring our ways must seem / to those for whom life is enough." Strange and devouring—and alien to our true nature. Rilke knows this, too; knows that the separation we feel is an illusion. The flowers would welcome us, he says, and we could "become one of them," if we "dreamed with them deeply." The poem gives us a way to enter that dream. Indeed, a shared dreaming might be the best definition of what poetry is and makes possible.

The closing lines of Valencia Robin's "Aubade with Sugar Maple" offer a wonderful example of such shared dreaming, an ecstatic sense of our essential interbeing, to use Thich Nhat Hanh's resonant term, with the earth:

And yet somehow that maple knew me. We talked
and talked until I became birched and oaked,
crabappled and cherried—drunk
with all the tree-ness I'd forgotten.
My God, to think—I could bud, even blossom.

A way of seeing the world that regards trees, and by extension all life forms, as sentient beings capable of some kind of knowing is revolutionary, subversive, and at the same time ancient and fundamental, a return to who we really are. It arises from truths our Paleolithic ancestors took as givens, intuitively if not self-consciously: that we are not separate from or more important than the other beings with whom we share this life; that we can communicate with them and they with us; that the earth itself is sacred, imbued with spirit and intelligence, aware of and responsive to our presence. And so in talking to the tree, in knowing that it knows her, the poet experiences a moment of awakening. Poets of earlier eras might have looked for the human qualities of the tree, but here Robin remembers "all the treeness" she "had forgotten" and becomes like a tree herself: "oaked," "crabappled," "cherried." And then she realizes to her astonishment that she could "bud, even blossom."

David Hinton's "Empty desert" gives us a vivid glimpse of what an experience of total non-separation might look like.

Empty desert
stretching away to the far
edge of

sight. Where

is this
person I
am? Gazing out
all morning, I find

nothing to be
but desert
gazing into desert. . .

When we see in this way, the self disappears. "Where
is this person I am?" Hinton asks, echoing the Bud-
dhist teaching that if you look for the self, you will
not find it, and you will not find it because it doesn't
exist. It is a construct, useful up to a point but ulti-
mately empty. Or the self loses all definition because
it encompasses the whole cosmos, an infinite net of

relationships. In *Wild Earth, Wild Mind: Our Place in the Sixth Extinction*, Hinton writes,

> The Cosmos evolved countless suns and planets; and here on our planet Earth, it evolved life-forms with image-forming eyes like ours. So what else is that gaze but the very Cosmos looking out at itself? What is thinking but the Cosmos contemplating itself? And our inexplicable love for this world, our delight and grief—what is that but the Cosmos loving itself, delighting in itself, grieving for itself?

Poetry's highest purpose is to remind us of our true nature, the untainted mirror-like mind that exists beneath our layers of conditioning, unchanging in the midst of constant change. Not a separate self, not an ego, but a wide-open, limitless awareness that flows throughout the cosmos and connects us to all things.

Like its predecessor, *The Poetry of Impermanence, Mindfulness, and Joy*, this collection can be randomly browsed, but reading the poems in order may be more rewarding, and more revealing. All the poems are strongly connected to each other, sometimes overtly, as in the sequence of elegiac poems for fathers that runs from Natasha Trethewey's "Elegy" to Yu Chang's "Old passport." Other connections are more subtle. For example, some version of not knowing—"I don't know," "all knowing ceased," "I did not yet know who I would become," "What we do not know lies in darkness"—appears throughout the group of poems that begins with W. S. Merwin's "For the Anniversary of My Death" and concludes with Danusha Laméris's "O Darkness." I did not plan or weave in that connecting thread; I was unaware of it myself until I had read through the section several times. Here and throughout the anthology, in choosing and arranging the poems, I allowed myself to be guided by an intuitive intelligence beyond my conscious knowing. Many such connections can be found in the book, but you'll likely miss them if you read the poems in isolation. These poems invite connection, embody connection, and are best experienced in their connections with each other.

In creating a space where the most powerful expressions of grief, gratitude, and reverence can be held and shared, the poems gathered here call us to remember our essential kinship with all life, to remember who we really are. Robert Major's haiku gives us a resonant image of such a space:

silent Friends meeting. . .
the sound of chairs being moved
to enlarge the circle

I like to think of this anthology as a similar kind of circle—a community, a sangha, a sacred meeting place—infinitely expandable to accommodate all who wish to enter. And my hope is that sustained imaginative engagement with these poems will help us move through the world more attuned to what we have lost, more grateful for what remains, and more reverent before the mystery and majesty of life itself.

BRINGING POETRY ONTO THE PATH

Just as there is no formula for making poems, there is no step-by-step guide for integrating poetry into our spiritual practice. I encourage you to experiment and find what works best for you. Maybe it's memorizing favorite poems and calling them to mind when you're standing in line or in need of the kind of sustenance poetry can provide; maybe it's simply reading and rereading a poem, reflecting on how it makes you feel, the memories it evokes, insights it sparks, how it illuminates different aspects of the Dharma; maybe it's savoring the pleasures a poem gives, its shape and textures and images, the way it moves and sounds, how the rhythms of its language flow into your own bodily rhythms of heart, breath, and sensation. The possibilities are many and varied.

One general rule that can be helpful and that I discuss in "The Art of Appreciative Attention" (in the appendix) and in *The Dharma of Poetry: How Poems Can Deepen Your Spiritual Practice and Open You to Joy*, is to approach the poems in an appreciative rather than interpretive mode, to let the analytical mind recede to the background and its proper supportive role while the more empathic, imaginative, intuitive mind comes into the foreground. Reading in this way, we let go of the need to control; we allow the poems to take us where they will. The end of Carl Dennis's "Canadian Hemlock" beautifully express this aspiration: "I want to be one of the witnesses of the familiar, / Open to revelation but not disposed / To insist on it." Again, see what works best for you, but above all, allow yourself to *enjoy* the poems and to love them fully when you find ones that speak to you with particular power.

If you would like to bring poems more directly into your practice, I have recorded a number of guided meditations that may be helpful. Throughout the book, QR codes will appear when a specific poem is available as a recording, and the recordings as a whole can be found at wisdomexperience.org/<tk>. Hearing a poem read aloud after a period of meditation can feel remarkably different—more resonant, more moving, more impactful—than simply reading it silently to yourself when you are in an ordinary state of mind. When you absorb a poem in the open, alert, highly sensitized state that meditation can induce, the words sink in more deeply, and we may experience the truth of what A. R. Ammons said, that "poetry is a verbal means to a non-verbal source," a way for language to take us beyond language, beyond thought, to something much richer and more mysterious.

I.
Grief

Downhearted

Six horses died in a tractor-trailer fire.
There. That's the hard part. I wanted
to tell you straight away so we could
grieve together. So many sad things,
that's just one on a long recent list
that loops and elongates in the chest,
in the diaphragm, in the alveoli. What
is it they say, heart-sick or downhearted?
I picture a heart lying down on the floor
of the torso, pulling up the blankets
over its head, thinking this pain will
go on forever (even though it won't).
The heart is watching Lifetime movies
and wishing, and missing all the good
parts of her that she has forgotten.
The heart is so tired of beating
herself up, she wants to stop it still,
but also she wants the blood to return,
wants to bring in the thrill and wind of the ride,

the fast pull of life driving underneath her.
What the heart wants? The heart wants
her horses back.

—*Ada Limón*

After a New Moon

Each evening you gaze in the southwest sky
as a crescent extends in argentine light.
When the moon was new, your mind was
desireless, but now both wax to the world.
While your neighbor's field is cleared,
your corner plot is strewn with desiccated
sunflower stalks. You scrutinize the bare
apricot limbs that have never set fruit,
the wisteria that has never blossomed,
and wince, hearing how, at New Year's,
teens bashed in a door and clubbed strangers.
Near a pond, someone kicks a dog out
of a pickup. Each second, a river edged
with ice shifts course. Last summer's
exposed tractor tire is nearly buried
under silt. An owl lifts from a poplar,
while the moon, no, the human mind
moves from brightest bright to darkest dark.

—*Arthur Sze*

Five Flights Up

Still dark.
The unknown bird sits on his usual branch.
The little dog next door barks in his sleep
inquiringly, just once.
Perhaps in his sleep, too, the bird inquires
once or twice, quavering.
Questions—if that is what they are—
answered directly, simply,
by day itself.

Enormous morning, ponderous, meticulous;
gray light streaking each bare branch,
each single twig, along one side,
making another tree, of glassy veins . . .
The bird still sits there. Now he seems to yawn.

The little black dog runs in his yard.
His owner's voice arises, stern,
"You ought to be ashamed!"
What has he done?
He bounces cheerfully up and down;
he rushes in circles in the fallen leaves.

Obviously, he has no sense of shame.
He and the bird know everything is answered,
all taken care of,
no need to ask again.
—Yesterday brought to today so lightly!
(A yesterday I find almost impossible to lift.)

—*Elizabeth Bishop*

Ice Storm

Unable to sleep, or pray, I stand
by the window looking out
at moonstruck trees a December storm
has bowed with ice.

Maple and mountain ash bend
under its glassy weight,
their cracked branches falling upon
the frozen snow.

The trees themselves, as in winters past,
will survive their burdening,
broken thrive. And am I less to You,
my God, than they?

—*Robert Hayden*

Sad Steps

Groping back to bed after a piss
I part thick curtains, and am startled by
The rapid clouds, the moon's cleanliness.

Four o'clock: wedge-shadowed gardens lie
Under a cavernous, a wind-picked sky.
There's something laughable about this,

The way the moon dashes through clouds that blow
Loosely as cannon-smoke to stand apart
(Stone-coloured light sharpening the roofs below)

High and preposterous and separate—
Lozenge of love! Medallion of art!
O wolves of memory! Immensements! No,

One shivers slightly, looking up there.
The hardness and the brightness and the plain
Far-reaching singleness of that wide stare

Is a reminder of the strength and pain
Of being young; that it can't come again,
But is for others undiminished somewhere.

—*Philip Larkin*

Anniversary

Exhausted by pity, I sit
in the sun near the pool.
The wind lifts the chimes
you repaired so patiently
last year, knotting the strings
from which the silver cylinders
depend. The sparrow I brought
home in my hand outlived you.
The stray white dog insisted on by
the clairvoyant came home following Annie.
Eighteen years. The chimes shudder
into sound. How reiterative is pity!
How suffering stares at itself—
rehearses its strophic voices.
He was so beautiful, they say.
The widow sits with her white dog,
listening to chimes. Eighteen
years. The ring on the finger,
placed there by you. The ringing,
touching rings—your careful
hands tying the knots holding
this bright appeal in place. The

fixed listening of self-pity—so unlike
this pure sound, this consciousness
of you, setting the chimes chiming
that they might last a lifetime—
here where the ring re-inscribes
itself as a circle of wind anticipated
not that long ago by your binding touch.

—*Carol Muske-Dukes*

reaching for green pears—
the pull
of an old scar

—*Peggy Willis Lyles*

spring sunshine
my dead wife's handprints
on the window pane

—*David Cobb*

The Five Stages of Grief

The night I lost you
someone pointed me towards
the Five Stages of Grief.
Go that way, they said,
it's easy, like learning to climb
stairs after the amputation.
And so I climbed.
Denial was first.
I sat down at breakfast
carefully setting the table
for two. I passed you the toast—
you sat there. I passed
you the paper—you hid
behind it.
Anger seemed more familiar.
I burned the toast, snatched
the paper and read the headlines myself.
But they mentioned your departure,
and so I moved on to
Bargaining. What could I exchange
for you? The silence
after storms? My typing fingers?

Before I could decide, *Depression*
came puffing up, a poor relation
its suitcase tied together
with string. In the suitcase
were bandages for the eyes
and bottles of sleep. I slid
all the way down the stairs
feeling nothing.
And all the time Hope
flashed on and off
in defective neon.
Hope was a signpost pointing
straight in the air.
Hope was my uncle's middle name,
he died of it.
After a year I am still climbing, though my feet slip
on your stone face.
The treeline
has long since disappeared;
green is a color
I have forgotten.
But now I see what I am climbing
towards: *Acceptance*
written in capital letters,
a special headline:

Acceptance
its name is in lights.
I struggle on,
waving and shouting.
Below, my whole life spreads its surf,
all the landscapes I've ever known
or dreamed of. Below
a fish jumps: the pulse
in your neck.
Acceptance. I finally
reach it.
But something is wrong.
Grief is a circular staircase.
I have lost you.

—*Linda Pastan*

Talking to Grief

Ah, Grief, I should not treat you
like a homeless dog
who comes to the back door
for a crust, for a meatless bone.
I should trust you.

I should coax you
into the house and give you
your own corner,
a worn mat to lie on,
your own water dish.

You think I don't know you've been living
under my porch.
You long for your real place to be readied
before winter comes. You need
your name,
your collar and tag. You need
the right to warn off intruders,
to consider

my house your own
and me your person
and yourself
my own dog.

—*Denise Levertov*

"oh antic God"

oh antic God
return to me
my mother in her thirties
leaned across the front porch
the huge pillow of her breasts
pressing against the rail
summoning me in for bed.

I am almost the dead woman's age times two.

I can barely recall her song
the scent of her hands
though her wild hair scratches my dreams
at night.   return to me, oh Lord of then
and now, my mother's calling,
her young voice humming my name.

—*Lucille Clifton*

Elegy

For my father

I think by now the river must be thick
    with salmon. Late August, I imagine it

as it was that morning: drizzle needling
    the surface, mist at the banks like a net

settling around us — everything damp
    and shining. That morning, awkward

and heavy in our hip waders, we stalked
    into the current and found our places —

you upstream a few yards and out
    far deeper. You must remember how

the river seeped in over your boots
    and you grew heavier with that defeat.

All day I kept turning to watch you, how
    first you mimed our guide's casting

then cast your invisible line, slicing the sky
between us; and later, rod in hand, how

you tried — again and again — to find
that perfect arc, flight of an insect

skimming the river's surface. Perhaps
you recall I cast my line and reeled in

two small trout we could not keep.
Because I had to release them, I confess,

I thought about the past — working
the hooks loose, the fish writhing

in my hands, each one slipping away
before I could let go. I can tell you now

that I tried to take it all in, record it
for an elegy I'd write — one day —

when the time came. Your daughter,
I was that ruthless. What does it matter

if I tell you I *learned* to be? You kept casting
your line, and when it did not come back

empty, it was tangled with mine. Some nights,
    dreaming, I step again into the small boat

that carried us out and watch the bank receding—
    my back to where I know we are headed.

—*Natasha Trethewey*

Swifts

For my father

Early fall, the light thin and brittle, and if
it's true that deprivation is a gift,
I accept the gift. I walk down
to Wallace Park to watch the swifts
that roost every September
in the Chapman School's tall
brick chimney. The charming swifts
with their long, forked tails
and swept-back wings,
ten thousand of them swerving
and darting in the evening sky,
a flowing, expandable spiral
of birds, clearing the air of insects
and riveting the wandering
human mind. Tonight there must be
three hundred spectators,
a whole hillside of us, ordinary people
whose wings fell off eons ago,
who traded flight for speech
and have regretted it ever since,

sodden and earth-bound as we are,
except for our lifted eyes, our *oohs* and *ahs*
that show we're still alive when
the peregrine falcon dives in
and knifes one out of the air,
which we boo or cheer,
sometimes simultaneously.
We love this passion play of form
and formlessness,
the birds' shifting patterns
flung out like a whiplash of water
or school of fish above
the stationary human school,
then drawn tight together,
a miracle they don't crash into each other,
a miracle of echo-location, until
you see them as they truly are:
a single organism, a body made mostly
of air and quick decisions, jagged
motions that gradually cohere—
a poem, in other words.
It takes the flock a full twenty minutes
to funnel down into the chimney,
and it seems a living smoke
pulled back into a still and sleeping fire,

so beautiful I forget for a moment
my father's death, or I turn my mind
away from it or, no, I open
my grief to accommodate this wonder
and wonder what he might have thought of it,
were we standing here together,
the kind of thing we never did, and now
will never do, except in my imagination—
that unchanging inner sky where the swifts
take flight whenever I want them to
and my father cannot die.

—*John Brehm*

Redemption Song

Finally fall
At last the mist,
heat's haze, we woke
these past weeks with

has lifted. We find
ourselves chill, a briskness
we hug ourselves in.
Frost greying the ground.

Grief might be easy
if there wasn't still
such beauty — would be far
simpler if the silver

maple didn't thrust
its leaves into flame,
trusting that spring
will find it again.

All this might be easier if
there wasn't a song
still lifting us above it,
if wind didn't trouble

my mind like water.
I half expect to see you
fill the autumn air
like breath—

At night I sleep
on clenched fists.
Days I'm like the child
who on the playground

falls, crying
not so much from pain
as surprise.
I'm tired of tide

taking you away,
then back again—
what's worse, the forgetting
or the thing

you can't forget.
Neither yet—
last summer's
choir of crickets

grown quiet.

—Kevin Young

Those Winter Sundays

Sundays too my father got up early
and put his clothes on in the blueblack cold,
then with cracked hands that ached
from labor in the weekday weather made
banked fires blaze. No one ever thanked him.

I'd wake and hear the cold splintering, breaking.
When the rooms were warm, he'd call,
and slowly I would rise and dress,
fearing the chronic angers of that house,

Speaking indifferently to him,
who had driven out the cold
and polished my good shoes as well.
What did I know, what did I know
of love's austere and lonely offices?

—*Robert Hayden*

Dangerous pavements. . .
but this year I face the ice
with my father's stick.

—*Seamus Heaney*

old passport
the tug
of my father's smile

—*Yu Chang*

Accidental Practitioners

In Wednesday night's class, the Introduction
to Forms & Techniques of Poetry, I'm teaching
as though we're on a small raft.
We are on a small raft.
We may never see the ones we love again.
Every poem is a message in a bottle.
Revision is urgency with tweezers.
How to pull out the bit not meant
to be there.
My brother died before midterm this term.
I have a student who has his name.
I call on this boy as often as I can.
I say his name aloud to alter
my relationship to grief.
I see you have your hand up, Sean.
I don't know if my brother ever read
a poem in his life. I worry I'm selling
poetry as salvation. Drinking and selling lines.
And in this same class I have a student
with my moved-out husband's name.
The husband-student doesn't raise his hand, speak.
And in this same class, a student with my

father's name. He sleeps in the back row.
I do not call out his name. I don't want to wake him.
I do not put them in the same group.
I spread them around. I watch myself
closely: be very fair to the husband.
He's done nothing wrong. He got scared.
Of what? Garden light and dying and death.
Of what? The interior experience. Not well lit!
After the midterm, I imagine they'll be
back to themselves: the students will
manage their own independent identities.
Already things are settling.
But my bite is not correct.
I'm dubious about the last stanza.
I walk in the evenings alone. I bought
a linen dress with horizontal stripes he'd hate.
I thought it would make me appear wider
in the sense of *unstoppable*.
But wearing stripes I just feel like I'm in jail.
I read into all hours. I dread seeing him weave
through town, rooms with women, his looky look.
I know "love" when simplified to its lowest
common denominator means *sorrow*
tomorrow. I know it isn't too late to change.

Tonight I'm introducing the English sonnet
as a method for containing anxiety, grief's pulse.
We sit on the floor. We write by hand.
One hundred and forty-four syllables.
I call on my father. I call on my brother.
We write the sonnets as letters
to the ones we have lost. I have never lost
anyone, my husband-student says,
out of the blue.
You can lose me, I tell him.
Pretend you will lose me.

—*Heather Sellers*

Mid-Term Break

I sat all morning in the college sick bay
Counting bells knelling classes to a close.
At two o'clock our neighbours drove me home.

In the porch I met my father crying—
He had always taken funerals in his stride—
And Big Jim Evans saying it was a hard blow.

The baby cooed and laughed and rocked the pram
When I came in, and I was embarrassed
By old men standing up to shake my hand

And tell me they were 'sorry for my trouble'.
Whispers informed strangers I was the eldest,
Away at school, as my mother held my hand

In hers and coughed out angry tearless sighs.
At ten o'clock the ambulance arrived
With the corpse, stanched and bandaged by the
    nurses.

Next morning I went up into the room. Snowdrops
And candles soothed the bedside; I saw him
For the first time in six weeks. Paler now,

Wearing a poppy bruise on his left temple,
He lay in the four-foot box as in his cot.
No gaudy scars, the bumper knocked him clear.

A four-foot box, a foot for every year.

—*Seamus Heaney*

Blind Red Bear

We found him under the bed when we moved in.
His eyes had been torn out by time
and his mouth was a thin, kinked string
of black thread ready to desert his face,
which was dirty white and, excepting the black nose,
the only part of him that was not stop-light red.
She loved him immediately with a hugging
delight that brought him with us

everywhere—to the movies, the zoo, the grocery,
the dentist. When she was a grown woman of twenty
she took him with her to Brazil.
After she died, the embassy shipped everything
back, and there he was among the books and clothes,
ragged and forlorn, like a single thought
of what was missing and would not be replaced,
like his eyes.

When she was small
I used to lie awake at night in that flimsy
beach house on the island and listen to her
in the next room telling him stories, talking about
her day. Then her voice would grow faint

and fainter, and I thought of them happily entering
the same dream,
just as I think of them now.

—*Christopher Howell*

Arabic

I don't remember the sounds
rising from below my breastbone
though I spoke that golden language
with the girls of Beirut, playing hopscotch
on the hot asphalt. We called out to our mothers
for lemonade, and when the men
walking home from work stooped down,
slipped us coins for candy, we thanked them.
At the market, I understood the bargaining
of the butcher, the vendors of fig and bread.
In Arabic, I whispered into the tufted ears
of a donkey, professing my love. And in Arabic
I sang at school, or dreamt at night.
There is an Arab saying,
Sad are only those who understand.
What did I know then of the endless trail
of losses? In the years that have passed,
I've buried a lover, a brother, a son.
At night, the low drumroll
of bombs eroded the edges of the city.
The girls? Who knows what has been taken
from them.

For a brief season I woke
to a man who would whisper to me
in Arabic, then tap the valley of my sternum,
ask me to repeat each word,
coaxing the rusty syllables from my throat.
See, he said, *they're still here.*
Though even that memory is faint.
And maybe he was right. What's gone
is not quite gone, but lingers.
Not the language, but the bones
of the language. Not the beloved,
but the dark bed the beloved makes
inside our bodies.

—*Danusha Laméris*

Autumn Passage

On suffering, which is real.
On the mouth that never closes,
the air that dries the mouth.

On the miraculous dying body,
its greens and purples.
On the beauty of hair itself.

On the dazzling toddler:
"Like eggplant," he says,
when you say "Vegetable,"

"Chrysanthemum" to "Flower."
On his grandmother's suffering, larger
than vanished skyscrapers,

September zucchini,
other things too big. For her glory
that goes along with it,

glory of grown children's vigil,
communal fealty, glory
of the body that operates

even as it falls apart, the body
that can no longer even make fever
but nonetheless burns

florid and bright and magnificent
as it dims, as it shrinks,
as it turns to something else.

—*Elizabeth Alexander*

So Good

Sing to me
weather about
one bird
peck, pecking
on bleached
winter grass.
March is here
like a granny
a child doesn't
like to kiss:
the farm smell,
a chill sweet-
ness. He'll
get over it.
March will pass
other birds
will sing in
other weather
time twists my
bent back.

A common cold.
And for no
reason my eyes
and the sky
fill with
tears. Two
kinds of
weather and
if you never
cry, well,
then you don't.
Snow that
turns to rain,
pain, physical
and emotive, too,
these pass. They
once weren't
here: they'll go
as Granny went
embanked in flowers
so long ago, so
cold a cheek to
ask a child

to kiss. "Those
birds," she
would have said,
"are starlings.
They came from
England." Or
"This is a
monarch buttter-
fly." Or, "That
is flypaper. Flies
spread germs."
Or. No. It
was all too long
ago and any
tears are for
the sullen day
suddenly so like
the inner life
that gutters,
burns and smokes.
Light the lights.
The day is dark
and where do
the starlings
sleep at night?

Good night, Granny,
so truly good.

—*James Schuyler*

Downpour

Last night we ended up on the couch
trying to remember
all of the friends who had died so far,

and this morning I wrote them down
in alphabetical order
on the flip side of a shopping list
you had left on the kitchen table.

So many of them had been swept away
as if by a hand from the sky,
it was good to recall them,
I was thinking
under the cold lights of a supermarket
as I guided a cart with a wobbly wheel
up and down the long strident aisles.

I was on the lookout for blueberries,
English muffins, linguini, heavy cream,
light bulbs, apples, Canadian bacon,
and whatever else was on the list,
which I managed to keep grocery side up,

until I had passed through the electric doors,
where I stopped to realize,
as I turned the list over,
that I had forgotten Terry O'Shea
as well as the bananas and the bread.

It was pouring by then,
spilling, as they say in Ireland,
people splashing across the lot to their cars.
And that is when I set out,
walking slowly and precisely,
a soaking-wet man
bearing bags of groceries,
walking as if in a procession honoring the dead.

I felt I owed this to Terry,
who was such a strong painter,
for almost forgetting him
and to all the others who had formed
a circle around him on the screen in my head.

I was walking more slowly now
in the presence of the compassion
the dead were extending to a comrade,

plus I was in no hurry to return
to the kitchen, where I would have to tell you
all about Terry and the bananas and the bread.

—*Billy Collins*

12/19/02

It seemed nothing would ever be the same
This feeling lasted for months
Not a day passed without a dozen mentions
of the devastation and the grief
Then life came back
it returned like sap to the tree
shooting new life into the veins
of parched leaves turning them green
and the old irritations came back,
they were life, too,
crowds pushing, taxis honking, the envies, the anger,
the woman who could not escape her misery
as she stood between two mirrored walls
couldn't sleep, took a pill, heard the noises of
   neighbors
the dogs barking, the pigeons in the alley yipping
   weirdly
and the phone that rang at eight twenty with the news
of Lucy's overdose we just saw her last Friday evening
at Jay's on Jane Street she'd been dead for a day or so
when they found her and there was no note
the autopsy's today the wake the day after tomorrow

and then I knew that life had resumed, ordinary
    bitching life
had come back

—*David Lehman*

Dutch Elm Disease

When Danny Johnson's big brother was killed in
    Vietnam,
Danny ran around the block five times. I counted.
    Ran
as if when he stopped his brother would be back in
    their driveway
washing his car. But nobody knew anything about
    time travel
back then, *Star Trek* hadn't even come out,
    Lieutenant Uhura
still on Broadway doing *Blues for Mr. Charlie*. And
    even if Danny
did understand the space-time continuum, his
    parents
weren't having it, his mother on the porch yelling
his name, his father tackling him on the front
    lawn, all us kids,
the whole block standing there on pause. Which
    didn't exist
either. No fast forward, no reverse. We weren't
    even Black

yet. Was Milwaukee even Milwaukee? Is the
    Lincoln Park Bridge
still there, do boys like Danny still climb over the
    rail,
hug their bony knees to their narrow chests and
    plop into the river
as if there's no way his parents could lose *two*
    children?
Which is all I know about Vietnam, that and the
    way the sun hung
in the faded sky as Danny ran around and around
and held the air hostage, that and the way the thick
    August air
ignored the leaves of all our doomed elm trees
and let itself be held hostage. The streets were like
    ghosts
when they cut down those trees.

—*Valencia Robin*

Song for the Turtles in the Gulf

We had been together so very long,
you willing to swim with me
just last month, myself merely small
in the ocean of splendor and light,
the reflections and distortions of us,
and now when I see the man from British Petroleum
lift you up dead from the plastic
bin of death,
he with a smile, you burned
and covered with red-black oil, torched
and pained, all I can think is that I loved your life,
the very air you exhaled when you rose,
old great mother, the beautiful swimmer,
the mosaic growth of shell
so detailed, no part of you
simple, meaningless,
or able to be created
by any human,
only destroyed.
How can they learn
the secret importance
of your beaten heart,

the eyes of another intelligence
than ours, maybe greater,
with claws, flippers, plastron.
Forgive us for being thrown off true,
for our trespasses,
in the eddies of the water
where we first walked.

—*Linda Hogan*

To the Field of Scotch Broom That Will Be Buried by the New Wing of the Mall

Half costume jewel, half parasite, you stood
swaying to the music of cash registers in the distance
while a helicopter chewed the linings
of the clouds above the clear-cuts.
And I forgave the pollen count
while cabbage moths teased up my hair
before your flowers fell apart when they
turned into seeds. How resigned you were
to your oblivion, unlistening to the cumuli
as they swept past. And soon those gusts
will mill you, when the backhoe comes
to dredge your roots, but that is not
what most impends, as the chopper descends
to the hospital roof so that somebody's heart
can be massaged back into its old habits.

Mine went a little haywire
at the crest of the road, on whose other side
you lay in blossom.

As if your purpose were to defibrillate me
with a thousand electrodes,
one volt each.

—*Lucia Perillo*

Flash Flood

I was making dinner, peeling radishes at the sink, when afternoon suddenly turned to pitch. Hail graveled against the windows.

Water rushed down my brick street, waves slung over the lawn—whitecaps in the garden.

From the porch, I watched sear-white rods fasten fire to the water. My spine bristled and I wondered if I'd been hit.

Evening cut loose as liquid. The strong sense of sailing away.

A grey sedan, stalled in the lake of my lawn, held a woman waving, window down, her voice sucked into the storm.

Do you want me to call someone? Lightning broke wild around my words and I felt like a powerful god speaking in pointless thunderbolts. She held her phone high, pointed to it.

Later, those two women or two other women waded down the street through knee high water, into the remnants.

From this water come electric snakes, chemical blooms, the new world.

The empty silver car bobbed against the palm on the boulevard.

Later, inside, I lay in clear cool water in the old green bath as monks sang the Ordinary—struck by music's aqueous pauses and silvering—until we lost power.

—*Heather Sellers*

She Told Me the Earth Loves Us

She said it softly, without a need
for conviction or romance.
After everything? I asked, ashamed.

That's not the kind of love she meant.
She walked through a field of gray
beetle-pored pine, snags branching

like polished bone. I forget sometimes
how trees look at me with the generosity
of water. I forget all the other

breath I'm breathing in.
Today I learned that trees can't sleep
with our lights on. That they knit

a forest in their language, their feelings.
This is not a metaphor.
Like seeing a face across a crowd,

we are learning all the old things,
newly shined and numbered.
I'm always looking

for a place to lie down
and cry. Green, mossed, shaded.
Or rock-quiet, empty. Somewhere

to hush and start over.
I put on my antlers in the sun.
I walk through the dark gates of the trees.

Grief waters my footsteps, leaving
a trail that glistens.

—*Anne Haven McDonnell*

Traveling through the Dark

Traveling through the dark I found a deer
dead on the edge of the Wilson River road.
It is usually best to roll them into the canyon:
that road is narrow; to swerve might make more
    dead.

By glow of the tail-light I stumbled back of the car
and stood by the heap, a doe, a recent killing;
she had stiffened already, almost cold.
I dragged her off; she was large in the belly.

My fingers touching her side brought me the
    reason—
her side was warm; her fawn lay there waiting,
alive, still, never to be born.
Beside that mountain road I hesitated.

The car aimed ahead its lowered parking lights;
under the hood purred the steady engine.
I stood in the glare of the warm exhaust turning red;
around our group I could hear the wilderness
    listen.

I thought hard for us all—my only swerving—,
then pushed her over the edge into the river.

—*William Stafford*

The Mower

The mower stalled, twice; kneeling, I found
A hedgehog jammed up against the blades,
Killed. It had been in the long grass.

I had seen it before, and even fed it, once.
Now I had mauled its unobtrusive world
Unmendably. Burial was no help:

Next morning I got up and it did not.
The first day after a death, the new absence
Is always the same; we should be careful

Of each other, we should be kind
While there is still time.

—*Philip Larkin*

dead roadside deer
a snowflake melts
on its open eye

—*George Swede*

in the silent movie
a bird I think extinct
is singing

—*LeRoy Gorman*

II.

Gratitude

First Spring–Like Day

Sitting at the open window
a few late birds
sun going down

orange ball in the west
purple around it, pinks
oranges, violets

colors only nature
and painters of velvet use
and in the background being ignored

just for a few minutes—forgive me—
the grinding machinery of life
the siren call of grief

—Greg Kosmicki

Concurrence

Each day's terror, almost
a form of boredom—madmen
at the wheel and
stepping on the gas and
the brakes no good—
and each day one,
sometimes two, morning-glories,
faultless, blue, blue sometimes
flecked with magenta, each
lit from within with
the first sunlight.

—*Denise Levertov*

Try to Praise the Mutilated World

Try to praise the mutilated world.
Remember June's long days,
and wild strawberries, drops of wine, the dew.
The nettles that methodically overgrow
the abandoned homesteads of exiles.
You must praise the mutilated world.
You watched the stylish yachts and ships;
one of them had a long trip ahead of it,
while salty oblivion awaited others.
You've seen the refugees heading nowhere,
you've heard the executioners sing joyfully.
You should praise the mutilated world.
Remember the moments when we were together
in a white room and the curtain fluttered.
Return in thought to the concert where music
    flared.
You gathered acorns in the park in autumn
and leaves eddied over the earth's scars.
Praise the mutilated world

and the gray feather a thrush lost,
and the gentle light that strays and vanishes
and returns.

—*Adam Zagajewski, translated from the Polish by Clare Cavanagh*

Evening

Moonlight pours down
without mercy, no matter
how many have perished
beneath the trees.

The river rolls on.

There will always be
silence, no matter
how long someone
has wept against
the side of a house,
bare forearms pressed
to the shingles.

Everything ends.
Even pain, even sorrow.

The swans drift on.

Reeds bear the weight
of their feathery heads.
Pebbles grow smaller,
smoother beneath night's

rough currents. We walk

long distances, carting
our bags, our packages.
Burdens or gifts.

We know the land
is disappearing beneath
the sea, islands swallowed
like prehistoric fish.
We know we are doomed,
done for, damned, and still
the light reaches us, falls
on our shoulders even now,

even here where the moon is
hidden from us, even though
the stars are so far away.

—*Dorianne Laux*

At Least

I want to get up early one more morning,
before sunrise. Before the birds, even.
I want to throw cold water on my face
and be at my work table
when the sky lightens and smoke
begins to rise from the chimneys
of the other houses.
I want to see the waves break
on this rocky beach, not just hear them
break as I did all night in my sleep.
I want to see again the ships
that pass through the Strait from every
seafaring country in the world—
old, dirty freighters just barely moving along,
and the swift new cargo vessels
painted every color under the sun
that cut the water as they pass.
I want to keep an eye out for them.
And for the little boat that plies
the water between the ships
and the pilot station near the lighthouse.
I want to see them take a man off the ship

and put another up on board.
I want to spend the day watching this happen
and reach my own conclusions.
I hate to seem greedy—I have so much
to be thankful for already.
But I want to get up early one more morning,
 at least.
And go to my place with some coffee and wait.
Just wait, to see what's going to happen.

—*Raymond Carver*

Gift

A day so happy.
Fog lifted early, I worked in the garden.
Hummingbirds were stopping over honeysuckle
    flowers.
There was no thing on earth I wanted to possess.
I knew no one worth my envying him.
Whatever evil I had suffered, I forgot.
To think that once I was the same man did not
    embarrass me.
In my body I felt no pain.
When straightening up, I saw the blue sea and
    sails.

—*Czesław Miłosz, translated from the Polish
by Robert Hass and the author*

Along the Willamette

April 2021

At the river's edge some kind of grassy plant
I can't identify and detritus I can:
two blue almost collapsed helium balloons
and a silver one a foot or so above the water,
fighting to get away, its birthday message
in red, block letters for someone named Kate,
their strings tangled together in the river.

All year during COVID I'd stayed away,
but this morning, the air sweet and cool,
I wandered the six blocks to the river,
wanting an hour of my old life back:
my routine of walking the wide path,
maybe a few gulls, persistent pigeons,
early morning runners, people on bikes.

Everything I asked for is here.
And now the sun, held back by fat,
white clouds when I left my apartment,
breaks through, lighting the water.
Almost on cue, five kayaks paddle by

causing a rush of waves to knock
and knock against the bank, releasing
the silver balloon, which rises
into the bluing sky, and a dozen geese
in that familiar vee I've missed,
their long, black necks stretched
into exclamation marks above it, honk
almost in unison as if to celebrate.
"Happy birthday, Kate," I say, happy
myself not to be anywhere else.

—*Andrea Hollander*

cherry petals
a child adds a handful
to the busker's cap

—*Christopher Herold*

crowd of umbrellas
a child opens his
face to the rain

—*Connie Donleycott*

Canadian Hemlock

Nothing is improved by being praised.
But that doesn't mean the bestowing of praise
On whatever deserves it isn't a useful calling
Even if no one is listening at the moment,
If I'm alone now on my morning walk,
Waiting at the corner of Bryant and Richmond
For the light to change, open to the company
Of this stunted hemlock on the strip of grass
Between sidewalk and curb. A gnarled hemlock
Barely five feet tall, which I must have passed
A thousand times without remarking,
And may forget to observe in the future.
So this seems the moment to note that whatever
Fungus or parasite has besieged it has failed
To thwart its efforts to continue.
I don't want to claim too much, to project
Emotions upon it that it does't feel.
But I don't want to praise too little, to deny
It possesses the green equivalent of fortitude
For fighting an invader to a standstill,
Just as I wouldn't want to limit my motive
For taking my morning walk to a need for exercise.

I want to be one of the witnesses of the familiar,
Open to revelation but not disposed
To insist on it. Let the tree withhold
What it wants to withhold. Let me see
What I'm ready to see now
When I set aside the notion that more is coming,
More reserved for some other day.

—*Carl Dennis*

The Young Sycamore

I must tell you
this young tree
whose round and firm trunk
between the wet

pavement and the gutter
(where water
is trickling) rises
bodily

into the air with
one undulant
thrust half its height—
and then

dividing and waning
sending out
young branches on
all sides—

hung with cocoons
it thins
till nothing is left of it
but two

eccentric knotted
twigs
bending forward
hornlike at the top

—*William Carlos Williams*

Ode to Everything

Somehow I have never thought
to thank the ice cream cone
for building a paradise in my mouth,
and can you believe I have never
thought to thank the purple trout lily
for demonstrating its six-petaled dive
or the yellow circle in a traffic light
for illustrating patience. My bad.
In my life, I have failed to praise
the postman whose loyalty is epic,
the laundress who treasures my skinny jeans
and other garments, and the auto repairman
who clangs a wrench inside my car tightening
her own music. Were my name called and I
were summoned on a brightly lit stage to accept
a little statuette, after staring in utter
disbelief, I would thank my dentist
as well as my neighbor who sits vigil
beside the dying far away from the lights,
and my fourth grade teacher who brought
down three-taped rulers on my hands
as punishment for daydreaming out a window

during an exam I already completed. Mea culpa.
Now that I know the value of the peaks
across from Flanders Hill, I will also perennially
    express
reverence for their green crowns.
I will never fail again to say small devotions for
the scar on a friend's face that lengthens
when I walk into a room.

—*Major Jackson*

Among the Multitudes

I am who I am.
A coincidence no less unthinkable
than any other.

I could have different
ancestors, after all,
I could have fluttered
from another nest
or crawled bescaled
from under another tree.

Nature's wardrobe
holds a fair supply of costumes:
spider, seagull, field mouse.
Each fits perfectly right off
and is dutifully worn
into shreds.

I didn't get a choice either,
but I can't complain.
I could have been someone
much less separate.

Someone from an anthill, shoal, or buzzing swarm,
an inch of landscape tousled by the wind.

Someone much less fortunate,
bred for my fur
or Christmas dinner,
something swimming under a square of glass.

A tree rooted to the ground
as the fire draws near.

A grass blade trampled by a stampede
of incomprehensible events.

A shady type whose darkness
dazzled some.

What if I'd prompted only fear,
loathing,
or pity?

If I'd been born
in the wrong tribe,
with all roads closed before me?

Fate has been kind
to me thus far.

I might never have been given
the memory of happy moments.

My yen for comparison
might have been taken away.

I might have been myself minus amazement,
that is,
someone completely different.

—*Wisława Szymborska*

Thanks

Thanks for the tree
between me & a sniper's bullet.
I don't know what made the grass
sway seconds before the Viet Cong
raised his soundless rifle.
Some voice always followed,
telling me which foot
to put down first.
Thanks for deflecting the ricochet
against that anarchy of dusk.
I was back in San Francisco
wrapped up in a woman's wild colors,
causing some dark bird's love call
to be shattered by daylight
when my hands reached up
& pulled a branch away
from my face. Thanks
for the vague white flower
that pointed to the gleaming metal
reflecting how it is to be broken
like mist over the grass,
as we played some deadly

game for blind gods.
What made me spot the monarch
writhing on a single thread
tied to a farmer's gate,
holding the day together
like an unfingered guitar string,
is beyond me. Maybe the hills
grew weary & leaned a little in the heat.
Again, thanks for the dud
hand grenade tossed at my feet
outside Chu Lai. I'm still
falling through its silence.
I don't know why the intrepid
sun touched the bayonet,
but I know that something
stood among those lost trees
& moved only when I moved.

—*Yusef Komunyakaa*

Ode to Fat

Tonight, as you undress, I watch your wondrous
flesh that's swelled again, the way a river swells
when the ice relents. Sweet relief
just to regard the sheaves of your hips,
your boundless breasts and marshy belly.
I adore the leverage
of your thighs and praise the promising
planets of your ass.
O, you were lean that terrifying year
you were unraveling, as though you were returning
to the slender scrap of a girl I fell in love with.
But your skin was vacant, a ripped sack,
sugar spilling out and your bones insistent.
O, praise the loyalty of the body
that labors to rebuild its palatial realm.
Bless butter. Bless brie.
Sanctify schmaltz. And cream and cashews.
Stoke the furnace
of the stomach and load the vessels. Darling,
drench yourself in opulent oil,

the lamp of your body glowing. May you always
flourish enormous and sumptuous,
be marbled with fat, a great vault that
I can enter, the cathedral where I pray.

—*Ellen Bass*

After Dürer

As when icy illness ends that you never expected
    Could possibly end, and the terrified body,
      enveloped
In warm water, reposes, you could kiss every child
    on the hand,
      Every leaf in the forest, every stone of the
      wall. A low moan escapes
The mouth. Melancholia, the accompanying
    spirit, is departing with
      Her ratty wings and crusted eyes, her suitcase
      of rocks.
A shy, small creature steps trembling from the
    brush.

—Emily Fragos

Realism

We are not so badly off, if we can
Admire Dutch painting. For that means
We shrug off what we have been told
For a hundred, two hundred years. Though we lost
Much of our previous confidence. Now we agree
That those trees outside the window, which
    probably exist,
Only pretend to greenness and treeness
And that the language loses when it tries to cope
With clusters of molecules. And yet, this here:
A jar, a tin plate, a half-peeled lemon,
Walnuts, a loaf of bread, last—and so strongly
It is hard not to believe in their lastingness.
And thus abstract art is brought to shame,
Even if we do not deserve any other.
Therefore I enter those landscapes
Under a cloudy sky from which a ray
Shoots out, and in the dark plains
A spot of brightness glows. Or the shore
With huts, boats, and on yellowish ice
Tiny figures skating. All this
is here eternally, just because once it was.

Splendor (certainly incomprehensible)
Touches a cracked wall, a refuse heap,
The floor of an inn, jerkins of the rustics,
A broom, and two fish bleeding on a board.
Rejoice! Give thanks! I raised my voice
To join them in their choral singing,
Amid their ruffles, collets, and silk shirts,
One of them already, who vanished long ago,
And our song soared up like smoke from a censer.

—*Czesław Miłosz, translated from the Polish*
  by Robert Hass and the author

A Cold Spring

for Jane Dewey, Maryland

Nothing is so beautiful as spring. —*Hopkins*

A cold spring:
the violet was flawed on the lawn.
For two weeks or more the trees hesitated;
the little leaves waited,
carefully indicating their characteristics.
Finally a grave green dust
settled over your big and aimless hills.
One day, in a chill white blast of sunshine,
on the side of one a calf was born.
The mother stopped lowing
and took a long time eating the after-birth,
a wretched flag,
but the calf got up promptly
and seemed inclined to feel gay.

The next day
was much warmer.
Greenish-white dogwood infiltrated the wood,
each petal burned, apparently, by a cigarette-butt;

and the blurred redbud stood
beside it, motionless, but almost more
like movement than any placeable color.
Four deer practiced leaping over your fences.
The infant oak-leaves swung through the sober oak.
Song-sparrows were wound up for the summer,
and in the maple the complementary cardinal
cracked a whip, and the sleeper awoke,
stretching miles of green limbs from the south.
In his cap the lilacs whitened,
then one day they fell like snow.
Now, in the evening,
a new moon comes.
The hills grow softer. Tufts of long grass show
where each cow-flop lies.
The bull-frogs are sounding,
slack strings plucked by heavy thumbs.
Beneath the light, against your white front door,
the smallest moths, like Chinese fans,
flatten themselves, silver and silver-gilt
over pale yellow, orange, or gray.
Now, from the thick grass, the fireflies
begin to rise:
up, then down, then up again:
lit on the ascending flight,

drifting simultaneously to the same height,
—exactly like the bubbles in champagne.
—Later on they rise much higher.
And your shadowy pastures will be able to offer
these particular glowing tributes
every evening now throughout the summer.

—*Elizabeth Bishop*

What Meets the Eye

Trash in the yards
white as early flowers,
the flash of aluminum cans
in broad sweeps
spilling down the embankments
to the shelter of rusty bedsprings
and the creosote fat of old tires,
the brawl of oil drums.
Now and again, the bold spread
of a car dump fans out,
then closes with the single shell
of an orange Vega, fastened
like a mutant insect to the slope.

Something almost yields.
It's that week before the flash of shoots
and the blue rush of Texas wild flowers.
Hawks on the updraft;
pockets of sky reflecting water.
It's that season of unreasonable hope,

when flocks of starlings
pulse up in a single motion
then scatter like a handful of grain
flung out over the fields.

—*Ruth Stone*

keep out sign
but the violets keep on
going

—*John Wills*

Oh I am zestful
in this field of grasses
openmouthed for rain.

—*Edith Shiffert*

Putting in the Seed

You come to fetch me from my work to-night
When supper's on the table, and we'll see
If I can leave off burying the white
Soft petals fallen from the apple tree
(Soft petals, yes, but not so barren quite,
Mingled with these, smooth bean and wrinkled pea);
And go along with you ere you lose sight
Of what you came for and become like me,
Slave to a Springtime passion for the earth.
How Love burns through the Putting in the Seed
On through the watching for that early birth
When, just as the soil tarnishes with weed,
The sturdy seedling with arched body comes
Shouldering its way and shedding the earth crumbs.

—*Robert Frost*

From Blossoms

From blossoms comes
this brown paper bag of peaches
we bought from the boy
at the bend in the road where we turned toward
signs painted *Peaches*.

From laden boughs, from hands,
from sweet fellowship in the bins,
comes nectar at the roadside, succulent
peaches we devour, dusty skin and all,
comes the familiar dust of summer, dust we eat.

O, to take what we love inside,
to carry within us an orchard, to eat
not only the skin, but the shade,
not only the sugar, but the days, to hold
the fruit in our hands, adore it, then bite into
the round jubilance of peach.

There are days we live
as if death were nowhere
in the background; from joy
to joy to joy, from wing to wing,
from blossom to blossom to
impossible blossom, to sweet impossible blossom.

—*Li-Young Lee*

June 30, 1974

for Jane and Joe Hazan

Let me tell you
that this weekend Sunday
morning in the country
fills my soul
with tranquil joy:
the dunes beyond
the pond beyond
the humps of bayberry—
my favorite shrub (today,
at least)—are
silent as a mountain
range: such a
subtle profile
against a sky that
goes from dawn
to blue. The roses
stir, the grapevine
at one end of the deck
shakes and turns
its youngest leaves

so they show pale
and flower-like.
A redwing blackbird
pecks at the grass;
another perches on a bush.
Another way, a millionaire's
white chateau turns
its flank to catch
the risen sun. No
other houses, except
this charming one,
alive with paintings,
plants and quiet.
I haven't said
a word. I like
to be alone
with friends. To get up
to this morning view
and eat poached eggs
and extra toast with
Tiptree Goosberry Preserve
(green)—and coffee,
milk, no sugar. Jane
said she heard
the freeze-dried kind

is healthier when
we went shopping
yesterday and she
and John bought
crude blue Persian plates.
How can coffee be
healthful? I mused
as sunny wind
streamed in the car
window driving home.
Home! How lucky to
have one, how arduous
to make this scene
of beauty for
your family and
friends. Friends!
How we must have
sounded, gossiping at
the dinner table
last night. Why, *that*
dinner table is
this breakfast table:
"The boy in trousers
is not the same boy
in no trousers," who

said? Discontinuity
in all we see and are:
the same, yet change,
change, change. "Inez,
it's good to see you."
Here comes the cat, sedate,
that killed and brought
a goldfinch yesterday.
I'd like to go out
for a swim but
it's a little cool
for that. Enough to
sit here drinking coffee,
writing, watching the clear
day ripen (such
a rainy June we had)
while Jane and Joe
sleep in their room
and John in his. I
think I'll make more toast.

—*James Schuyler*

Morning

Why do we bother with the rest of the day,
the swale of the afternoon,
the sudden dip into evening,

then night with his notorious perfumes,
his many-pointed stars?

This is the best—
throwing off the light covers,
feet on the cold floor,
and buzzing around the house on espresso—

maybe a splash of water on the face,
a palmful of vitamins—
but mostly buzzing around the house on espresso,

dictionary and atlas open on the rug,
the typewriter waiting for the key of the head,
a cello on the radio,

and, if necessary, the windows—
trees fifty, a hundred years old
out there,
heavy clouds on the way

and the lawn steaming like a horse
in the early morning.

—*Billy Collins*

Morning, East Wallingford

Morning in East Wallingford,
not to be confused with
Wallingford proper,
down the road
a few miles
here in Vermont:
a bifurcated village.
Nothing much is
happening.
We had a thunderstorm
last night and now
bullfrogs are squawking
from the pond, as if
the storm had lodged
fragments of thunder
in their throats,
a wet and rubbery sound,
mildly insistent,
counterpointed by
faint birdsong
against a backdrop
of highway traffic,

cars and trucks,
the human contribution
to the soundscape.
The luna moth
we found last night
affixed to the porch railing
is gone, swept away by
the wind probably.
A fabulous creature,
green and leaflike,
with delicate orange ferns
for antennae, and a curlicue
on each wing, added
for what purpose?
A mystery.
My wife is asleep upstairs,
her mother and father
a little further down the road.
I sit here feeling content,
even as I know the world
as we know it is ending—
happiness resting
in the pit of my stomach,
a calm excitement,
my mind free of anger,

resentment, ambition, regret.
Twelve raindrops hang
from the window sash,
gathering weight.
One or two look ready
to fall, but who
knows when
that will happen.
Pearled, light-filled,
each one a condensation
of cloud called downward
by invisible forces
just as we are,
falling but not yet fallen,
held between earth
and sky, then and now,
and now the rain begins again.

—*John Brehm*

a great blue heron
shakes rain from his wings
then passes through it

—*Margaret Chula*

after the rain
a white butterfly
on the clothesline

—*George Swede*

Bus 14, Downtown to
Southeast 34th and Hawthorne

The sun hot on my shoulders, the bus stop crowded,
the bus, full when it reaches us and now fuller,
pulls east toward the Hawthorne Bridge
and more east across the hectic street
where more and more cars slow the traffic,
and I try not to sway as I stand in the aisle,
one arm up to grasp the grab bar,
the other around the bouquet
from Gifford's I hover over
like the mother of a newborn,
at each stop the aisle growing
calmer, emptier, and most of us
relieved enough at our departure
to shout thanks to the driver
whose face I forget altogether
as the sun glints off the Bagdad Theater
and I step off the bus and leave the sound
of all that traffic behind and turn down
this residential street that grows
quieter and a little bit cooler
while I move beneath tulip trees

no longer in bloom although
snapdragons and hollyhocks rise
like an entourage on either side
of the sidewalk the closer I get
to the dinner Suzanne has been making
all day in her kitchen, the bouquet I carry
quite unharmed, the freesias I wanted
so out of season the clerk pulled
three blue hydrangeas from a pail,
then from a glass-doored cooler
four yellow roses, and wrapped them
together in a funnel of plain tan paper,
the scent of the roses just as I reach
Suzanne and Robert's house
overtaken by the odor
of simmering curry that strays
through the screen door
and out onto the porch
to greet me.

—*Andrea Hollander*

Bottle of Wine

I like to park a few blocks from the house of my hosts
And walk with my bottle of wine the tree-lined streets,
Anticipating the dinner with friends that awaits me.
A bottle of wine showing not only that I'm grateful
To be included but that I'm eager to do my part,
To offer a gift that won't survive the evening,
That says I've set aside the need for transcendence
And made my peace at last with living in time.
Soon we'll welcome the evening with a toast.
Soon we'll be toasting it in farewell
As it starts on its journey into the near past
And then the far. Do the houses I'm passing
Regard me as a creature about to vanish
Into the realm of shadow while they have resolved
To hold their ground? But the bottle I'm carrying
Shows how the past can enhance the present.
The grapes it was made from were plucked and
     pressed
Seven years ago in a vineyard in Burgundy
According to customs already in place for generations
By the time these houses moved from the realm
Of blueprints and estimates into brick and wood.

The bottle will testify that traditions once honored
Are being adhered to still, with patience, with pride.
And if the past is present this evening, isn't the future
Present as well in the thought that the ritual
I'm helping to pass along will prove enduring,
That however much the world around it may alter,
Guests will still perform it in eras to come?
I hope I feel their presence in spirit
Under these trees later this evening
As I walk back to my car with empty hands.

—*Carl Dennis*

Thanksgiving

When the sun spilled its luster on the front walk,
day became epoch—swelling into ceremony.

My mother trimmed the last of the year's roses,
my father the hedges staged about the house.

Rolling thorn and twine up to the ridge of woods,
I heaped their fine work where the dead

spent grass of summer lay. Fragments of body
spread wide like wings—each cartful, a burial

then bardo. Though I thought it quixotic,
I returned by turns for more of the fallen. A wind

carried me across the yard, sliding over the blood
maples. A lifeforce unreeled, not of me—no

but through me. Strange and severe, like a slow
storm it consumed me. And no one knew

of all this pomp, except two deer who stopped
to consider it: one doe, one buck, white scuts at rest.

I considered them, catching my breath—and then
went down again, round and round, helpless

until the frontage was stark: the eaves proud,
vases full, and we were ready for winter.

—*Alan Yan*

Thanks

Listen
with the night falling we are saying thank you
we are stopping on the bridges to bow from the
    railings
we are running out of the glass rooms
with our mouths full of food to look at the sky
and say thank you
we are standing by the water thanking it
standing by the windows looking out
in our directions

back from a series of hospitals back from a mugging
after funerals we are saying thank you
after the news of the dead
whether or not we knew them we are saying thank you

over telephones we are saying thank you
in doorways and in the backs of cars and in elevators
remembering wars and the police at the door
and the beatings on stairs we are saying thank you
in the banks we are saying thank you
in the faces of the officials and the rich

and of all who will never change
we go on saying thank you thank you

with the animals dying around us
our lost feelings we are saying thank you
with the forests falling faster than the minutes
of our lives we are saying thank you
with the words going out like cells of a brain
with the cities growing over us
we are saying thank you faster and faster
with nobody listening we are saying thank you
we are saying thank you and waving
dark though it is

—*W. S. Merwin*

III.

Reverence

Return

A little too abstract, a little too wise,
It is time for us to kiss the earth again,
It is time to let the leaves rain from the skies,
Let the rich life run to the roots again.
I will go to the lovely Sur Rivers
And dip my arms in them up to the shoulders.
I will find my accounting where the alder leaf
    quivers
In the ocean wind over the river boulders.
I will touch things and things and no more thoughts,
That breed like mouthless May-flies darkening
    the sky,
The insect clouds that blind our passionate hawks
So that they cannot strike, hardly can fly.
Things are the hawk's food and noble is the
    mountain, Oh noble
Pico Blanco, steep sea-wave of marble.

—*Robinson Jeffers*

See the Flowers

See the flowers, so faithful to Earth.
We know their fate because we share it.
Were they to grieve for their wilting,
that grief would be ours to feel.

There's a lightness in things. Only *we* move forever
    burdened,
pressing ourselves into everything, obsessed by weight.
How strange and devouring our ways must seem
to those for whom life is enough.

If you could enter their dreaming and dream with
    them deeply,
you would come back different to a different day,
moving so easily from that common depth.

Or maybe just stay there: they would bloom and
    welcome you,
all those brothers and sisters tossing in the meadows,
and you would be one of them.

*—Rainer Maria Rilke, translated from the
German by Joanna Macy and Anita Barrows*

Speaking Tree

I had a beautiful dream I was dancing with a tree.
—Sandra Cisneros

Some things on this earth are unspeakable:
Genealogy of the broken—
A shy wind threading leaves after a massacre,
Or the smell of coffee and no one there—

Some humans say trees are not sentient beings,
But they do not understand poetry—

Nor can they hear the singing of trees when they
    are fed by
Wind, or water music—
Or hear their cries of anguish when they are
    broken and bereft—

Now I am a woman longing to be a tree, planted in
    a moist, dark earth
Between sunrise and sunset—

I cannot walk through all realms—
I carry a yearning I cannot bear alone in the dark—

What shall I do with all this heartache?
The deepest-rooted dream of a tree is to walk
Even just a little ways, from the place next to the
  doorway—
To the edge of the river of life, and drink—

I have heard trees talking, long after the sun has
  gone down:

Imagine what would it be like to dance close together
In this land of water and knowledge. . .

To drink deep what is undrinkable.

—*Joy Harjo*

say no words
time is collapsing
in the woods

—*Sonia Sanchez*

summer evening
we turn out all the lights
to hear the rain

—*Peggy Willis Lyles*

The New Cosmology

So it's true: the poplar and I
are sisters, daughters of an ancient star,
every last thing

so much the same
(harp, toothpick, linnet, sleet)
that whatever I touch

is touching me, *whatever*
is a cousin,
unremote. Even the metaphors—

ruby as blood, blood
as river, river as dream—all are true,
just as the poets promised.

—*Paulann Petersen*

Milkweed

While I stood here, in the open, lost in myself,
I must have looked a long time
Down the corn rows, beyond grass,
The small house,
White walls, animals lumbering toward the barn.
I look down now. It is all changed.
Whatever it was I lost, whatever I wept for
Was a wild, gentle thing, the small dark eyes
Loving me in secret.
It is here. At a touch of my hand,
The air fills with delicate creatures
From the other world.

—*James Wright*

For the Anniversary of My Death

Every year without knowing it I have passed the day
When the last fires will wave to me
And the silence will set out
Tireless traveler
Like the beam of a lightless star

Then I will no longer
Find myself in life as in a strange garment
Surprised at the earth
And the love of one woman
And the shamelessness of men
As today writing after three days of rain
Hearing the wren sing and the falling cease
And bowing not knowing to what

—W. S. Merwin

Poetics

I look for the way
things will turn
out spiraling from a center,
the shape
things will take to come forth in

so that the birch tree white
touched black at branches
will stand out
wind-glittering
totally its apparent self:

I look for the forms
things want to come as

from what black wells of possibility,
how a thing will
unfold:

not the shape on paper—though
that, too—but the
uninterfering means on paper:

not so much looking for the shape
as being available
to any shape that may be
summoning itself
through me
from the self not mine but ours.

—*A. R. Ammons*

Poetry

And it was at that age . . . Poetry arrived
in search of me. I don't know, I don't know where
it came from, from winter or a river.
I don't know how or when,
no they were not voices, they were not
words, nor silence,
but from a street I was summoned,
from the branches of night,
abruptly from the others,
among violent fires
or returning alone,
there I was without a face
and it touched me.

I did not know what to say, my mouth
had no way
with names,
my eyes were blind,
and something started in my soul,
fever or forgotten wings,
and I made my own way,
deciphering

that fire,
and I wrote the first faint line,
faint, without substance, pure
nonsense,
pure wisdom
of someone who knows nothing,
and suddenly I saw
the heavens
unfastened
and open,
planets,

palpitating plantations,
shadow perforated,
riddled
with arrows, fire and flowers,
the winding night, the universe.

And I, infinitesimal being,
drunk with the great starry
void,
likeness, image of
mystery,

felt myself a pure part
of the abyss,
I wheeled with the stars,
my heart broke loose on the wind.

—*Pablo Neruda, translated from the Spanish by Alastair Reid*

A Meadow

It was a riverside meadow, lush from before the
    hay harvest,
On an immaculate day in the sun of June.
I searched for it, found it, recognized it.
Grasses and flowers grew there familiar in my
    childhood.
With half-closed eyelids I absorbed luminescence.
And the scent garnered me, all knowing ceased.
Suddenly I felt I was disappearing and weeping
    with joy.

—*Czesław Miłosz, translated from the Polish
  by Robert Hass and the author*

Praise Song for the Day

A Poem for Barack Obama's Presidential Inauguration

Each day we go about our business,
walking past each other, catching each other's
eyes or not, about to speak or speaking.

All about us is noise. All about us is
noise and bramble, thorn and din, each
one of our ancestors on our tongues.

Someone is stitching up a hem, darning
a hole in a uniform, patching a tire,
repairing the things in need of repair.

Someone is trying to make music somewhere,
with a pair of wooden spoons on an oil drum,
with cello, boom box, harmonica, voice.

A woman and her son wait for the bus.
A farmer considers the changing sky.
A teacher says, *Take out your pencils. Begin.*

We encounter each other in words, words
spiny or smooth, whispered or declaimed,
words to consider, reconsider.

We cross dirt roads and highways that mark
the will of some one and then others, who said
I need to see what's on the other side.

I know there's something better down the road.
We need to find a place where we are safe.
We walk into that which we cannot yet see.

Say it plain: that many have died for this day.
Sing the names of the dead who brought us here,
who laid the train tracks, raised the bridges,

picked the cotton and the lettuce, built
brick by brick the glittering edifices
they would then keep clean and work inside of.

Praise song for struggle, praise song for the day.
Praise song for every hand-lettered sign,
the figuring-it-out at kitchen tables.

Some live by *love thy neighbor as thyself*,
others by *first do no harm* or *take no more
than you need*. What if the mightiest word is love?

Love beyond marital, filial, national,
love that casts a widening pool of light,
love with no need to pre-empt grievance.

In today's sharp sparkle, this winter air,
any thing can be made, any sentence begun.
On the brink, on the brim, on the cusp,

praise song for walking forward in that light.

—*Elizabeth Alexander*

Overture

Portland, Oregon, February 2012

So I stepped off the streetcar
and walked to the bus stop,
marveling at the city around me,
and at the young woman I could never be
standing as if beautiful
with her tattooed neck
and metal studs through her nose and ears,
and actually she was beautiful,
singing a familiar tune, its notes of grace
filling the space between the two of us,
and suddenly too a limping man
with his cardboard WILL-WORK-FOR-FOOD sign
like the title of a poem and not his life,
but who was he then,
because he began to hum, and the woman,
teeth not yellow like his, smiling at him,
reached into the breast pocket
of her denim jacket while she sang,
and fluttered a five-dollar bill toward him
like some butterfly, which reminded me

of my mother, who sang on the bed of her death
as if song could keep her alive, or maybe
it was I who imagined this, a prayer
not for the dead but from the dying,
my mother in her purple gown
singing as if Death were not the name
of anything, but part of an overture,
her brown eyes earnest like those
of the woman at the bus stop in my new city
where I did not yet know who I would become
but now it seemed I was at least a singer
at a bus stop, for my own voice joined in
without my permission and the three of us hovered
in the mellifluous air on the darkening sidewalk
as the bus came to us and lifted us
together and away.

—*Andrea Hollander*

O Darkness

"My arm is so brown and so beautiful," is a
    thought I have
as I'm about to turn off the lamp and go to sleep.
I look at it a moment in the soft glow, and see it,
    briefly,
as though it belonged to someone else. A reddish
kind of brown, like a toasted almond, only flecked
with the fine, gold hairs of summer. And it occurs
    to me,
that I have always loved the brownness of my skin,
the way, just now, I stopped to admire my own thigh,
its deeper tone against the crisp white of my cotton
    robe.
As a girl, I wanted to be dark as my mother, whose
    skin
shone against crimson, malachite, plum. I loved
    the way
that gold gleamed against her neck, the way dark skin
forgives the accumulation of our years and griefs—
    and still
goes on, pliant and smooth and new. It made sense
    to me

that others slathered their limbs with oil, with
     unguent,
laid themselves out on roofs, on decks, on banks
     of sand,
gave themselves to the mercy of the sun. Though
     when
I seek a synonym for *dark*, I find *dim*, *nefarious*, *gloomy*,
threatening, *impure*. Is the world still so afraid of
     shadows?
Of the dark face of the earth, falling across the
     moon?
The dark earth, from which we've sprung, to
     which
we shall return? What we do not know lies in
     darkness.
The way the unsayable rests at the back of the
     tongue.
So let us sing of it—for the earth is a dark loam
and the night sky an unfathomable darkness.
And it is darkness I now praise. The dark at the
     exact
center of the eye. Dark in the bell's small cave.
The secret cavity of the nucleus. The quark.
How hidden is the sacred, quickening in the dark
behind the visible world. O Yaweh, O Jehovah,

henceforth I will name you: *Inkwell, Ear of Jaguar,
Skin of the Fig, Black Jade, Our Lady of Onyx.* That
which I cannot fathom. In whose image I am made.

—*Danusha Laméris*

Let This Darkness Be a Bell Tower

Quiet friend who has come so far,
feel how your breathing makes more space around
   you.
Let this darkness be a bell tower
and you the bell. As you ring,

what batters you becomes your strength.
Move back and forth into the change.
What is it like, such intensity of pain?
If the drink is bitter, turn yourself to wine.

In this uncontainable night,
be the mystery at the crossroads of your senses,
the meaning discovered there.

And if the world has ceased to hear you,
say to the silent earth: I flow.
To the rushing water, speak: I am.

—*Rainer Maria Rilke, translated by Joanna
   Macy and Anita Barrows*

Fern, Coal, Diamond

The intense pressure of the earth
makes coal out of ferns, diamonds out of coal.
The intense pressure of the earth
is within us, and makes coal
and diamond desires.

For instance, we are a river
flowing and flowing out to sea,
an oak fire flaring and flaring in a night
with no wind, or, protean,
a river, a fire, an oak, a hawk, a wind.

And, at first light,
I mark the stages of our growth:
mark fern, coal, diamond,
mark a pressure transforming
even broken nails and broken glass into
clear molten light.

—Arthur Sze

from Desert

Empty desert
stretching away to the far
edge of

sight. Where

is this
person I
am? Gazing out
all morning, I find

nothing to be
but desert
gazing into desert

desert

desert whispering its
own name
here in my
voice, whispering

sun and mountain
ridgeline, scrawled ocotillo
tipped in orange

bloom and blue
lightning-haunted sky.

—*David Hinton*

last night lightning
this morning
the white iris

—*Patricia Donegan*

Owl feather
      in my palm
            —the feel of moonlight

—*Vincent Tripi*

Daybreak

On the tidal mud, just before sunset,
dozens of starfishes
were creeping. It was
as though the mud were a sky
and enormous, imperfect stars
moved across it as slowly
as the actual stars cross heaven.
All at once they stopped,
and as if they had simply
increased their receptivity
to gravity, they sank down
into the mud, faded down
into it and lay still, and by the time
pink of sunset broke across them
they were as invisible
as the true stars at daybreak.

—*Galway Kinnell*

Over the Moon

Five a.m.—the soft percussion of the rain
on the slanted tin rooftop of my study.
I study it: a single drop dropping again
and again at one second intervals,
like the ticking of a watery clock
above my head. Off to my right,
it comes down in loose clusters,
an absentminded thrumming of fingers
on a tabletop, random, irregular,
or falling in a pattern I can't perceive.
It's too dark to see the rain as it falls,
only the reflection of my room
projected onto the empty space beyond
my *window*—an old Norse word
made from two other words: *wind* and *eye*.
My bookcases float blurrily
in the air above the alley,
I tap the keyboard and words appear,
and now the rain appears to be hesitating,
or reconsidering, though it will likely
fall all day long on the bamboo trees
I cannot see, the glorybower, the lilacs

and azaleas readying themselves,
summoning their flowers from the depths
of nonexistence, three kinds of Japanese
maples and the improbable ferns,
huge and flamelike, heart-shaped,
that edge the yard. Last night we stopped
and stepped backward when we crossed
a sidewalk puddle where the moon
had fallen between a reflection
of rootlike branches and swiftly
passing clouds to hover underneath us.
As above, so below, the old alchemists said,
everything mirroring everything else,
falling and rising and falling.
We lingered looking down, then
stepped over the moon and came home.

—*John Brehm*

Monet Refuses the Operation

Doctor, you say there are no haloes
around the streetlights in Paris
and what I see is an aberration
caused by old age, an affliction.
I tell you it has taken me all my life
to arrive at the vision of gas lamps as angels,
to soften and blur and finally banish
the edges you regret I don't see,
to learn that the line I called the horizon
does not exist and sky and water,
so long apart, are the same state of being.
Fifty-four years before I could see
Rouen cathedral is built
of parallel shafts of sun,
and now you want to restore
my youthful errors: fixed
notions of top and bottom,
the illusion of three-dimensional space,
wisteria separate
from the bridge it covers.

What can I say to convince you
the Houses of Parliament dissolve
night after night to become
the fluid dream of the Thames?
I will not return to a universe
of objects that don't know each other,
as if islands were not the lost children
of one great continent. The world
is flux, and light becomes what it touches,
becomes water, lilies on water,
above and below water,
becomes lilac and mauve and yellow
and white and cerulean lamps,
small fists passing sunlight
so quickly to one another
that it would take long, streaming hair
inside my brush to catch it.
To paint the speed of light!
Our weighted shapes, these verticals,
burn to mix with air
and change our bones, skin, clothes
to gases. Doctor,

if only you could see
how heaven pulls earth into its arms
and how infinitely the heart expands
to claim this world, blue vapor without end.

—*Lisel Mueller*

The Secret

Don't tell capitalism,
but I've learned the secret
value of wilting
on the sofa, both hands
vined around my head,
both ears invested
in the window bird
who dives through leaves
toward golden music
buried in the hedge
like treasure.

And don't tell your hedge
fund manager or his over
lords, but just by stealing
three deep breaths for
your own body, for your own
being, you'll be storing up
unspeakable wealth,
you'll be leaping clean

past retirement into the fire
of god—can you feel it,
warm against your hands,
the heaven of your life?

—*Justin Rigamonti*

Aubade with Sugar Maple

When the hard edges of the book
that sang me to sleep woke me
I assumed thoughts of all I hadn't accomplished
weren't far behind, the people I'd disappointed,
the money I hadn't made,
the power structure I'd rarely opposed.
But instead I found myself greeted
by an almost criminal hope, somehow free
of the social order that had shaped
my mind so that by the time the sun peeked in
and the huge sugar maple that filled my window
spoke, the only thing I questioned
was the forty hour work week, why the French
and Italians got *eight* weeks vacation.
Because it's been what—a million years?
And yet somehow that maple knew me. We talked
and talked until I became birched and oaked,
crabappled and cherried—drunk
with all the tree-ness I'd forgotten.
My God, to think—I could bud, even blossom.

—*Valencia Robin*

The Lake Isle of Innisfree

I will arise and go now, and go to Innisfree,
And a small cabin build there, of clay and wattles
   made:
Nine bean-rows will I have there, a hive for the
   honey-bee;
And live alone in the bee-loud glade.

And I shall have some peace there, for peace comes
   dropping slow,
Dropping from the veils of the morning to where
   the cricket sings;
There midnight's all a glimmer, and noon a purple
   glow,
And evening full of the linnet's wings.

I will arise and go now, for always night and day
I hear lake water lapping with low sounds by the shore;
While I stand on the roadway, or on the pavements
   grey,
I hear it in the deep heart's core.

—*William Butler Yeats*

The Peace of Wild Things

When despair for the world grows in me
and I wake in the night at the least sound
in fear of what my life and my children's lives may be,
I go and lie down where the wood drake
rests in his beauty on the water, and the great
   heron feeds.
I come into the peace of wild things
who do not tax their lives with forethought
of grief. I come into the presence of still water.
And I feel above me the day-blind stars
waiting with their light. For a time
I rest in the grace of the world, and am free.

—*Wendell Berry*

fallen leaves
the abbot sweeps
around them

—*John Brandi*

silent Friends meeting. . .
the sound of chairs being moved
to enlarge the circle

—*Robert Major*

Celebration

Brilliant, this day—a young virtuoso of a day.
Morning shadows cut by sharpest scissors,
deft hands. And every prodigy of green—
whether it's ferns or lichen or needles
or impatient points of bud on spindly bushes—
greener than ever before.
             And the way the conifers
hold new cones to the light for blessing,
a festive rite, and sing the oceanic chant the wind
transcribes for them!
A day that shines in the cold
like a first-prize brass band swinging along the street
of a coal-dusty village, wholly at odds
with the claims of reasonable gloom.

—*Denise Levertov*

Spring and All

By the road to the contagious hospital
under the surge of the blue
mottled clouds driven from the
northeast—a cold wind. Beyond, the
waste of broad, muddy fields
brown with dried weeds, standing and fallen

patches of standing water
the scattering of tall trees

All along the road the reddish
purplish, forked, upstanding, twiggy
stuff of bushes and small trees
with dead, brown leaves under them
leafless vines—

Lifeless in appearance, sluggish
dazed spring approaches—

They enter the new world naked,
cold, uncertain of all
save that they enter. All about them
the cold, familiar wind—

Now the grass, tomorrow
the stiff curl of wildcarrot leaf
One by one objects are defined—
It quickens: clarity, outline of leaf

But now the stark dignity of
entrance—Still, the profound change
has come upon them: rooted, they
grip down and begin to awaken

—*William Carlos Williams*

Still

I said I will find what is lowly
        and put the roots of my identity
        down there:
each day I'll wake up
and find the lowly nearby,
        a handy focus and reminder,
a ready measure of my significance,
the voice by which I would be heard,
the wills, the kinds of selfishness
        I could
freely adopt as my own:

but though I have looked everywhere,
        I can find nothing
        to give myself to:
        everything is

magnificent with existence, is in
surfeit of glory:
nothing is diminished,
nothing has been diminished for me:

I said what is more lowly than the grass:
    ah, underneath,
    a ground-crust of dry-burnt moss:
    I looked at it closely
and said this can be my habitat: but
nestling in I
found
    below the brown exterior
    green mechanisms beyond the intellect
awaiting resurrection in rain: so I got up
and ran saying there is nothing lowly in the
   universe:
I found a beggar:
he had stumps for legs: nobody was paying
him any attention: everybody went on by:
    I nestled in and found his life:
there, love shook his body like a devastation:
I said
    though I have looked everywhere
    I can find nothing lowly
    in the universe:

I whirled through transfigurations up and down,
transfigurations of size and shape and place:
     at one sudden point came still,
     stood in wonder:
moss, beggar, weed, tick, pine, self, magnificent
     with being!

—*A. R. Ammons*

Postscript

And some time make the time to drive out west
Into County Clare, along the Flaggy Shore,
In September or October, when the wind
And the light are working off each other
So that the ocean on one side is wild
With foam and glitter, and inland among stones
The surface of a slate-grey lake is lit
By the earthed lightning of a flock of swans,
Their feathers roughed and ruffling, white on white,
Their fully grown headstrong-looking heads
Tucked or cresting or busy underwater.
Useless to think you'll park and capture it
More thoroughly. You are neither here nor there,
A hurry through which known and strange things
    pass
As big soft buffetings come at the car sideways
And catch the heart off guard and blow it open.

—*Seamus Heaney*

Appendix

The Art of
Appreciative Attention

So much of our growth on the spiritual path comes not from gaining new knowledge but from remembering what we've always known but have forgotten. Not from learning but unlearning, clearing away the obscurations—the false beliefs and unexamined assumptions—that keep us from accessing our innate wisdom and living from our true nature. The poet Charles Wright puts it succinctly: "For knowledge, add, for wisdom, take away."

The same is true for poetry. Our first step is to let go of our preconceptions about what a poem is and how we should approach it. For example: the idea that poems are little more than verbal mechanisms—sometimes frustratingly elusive ones—for delivering meaning. Once we let go of that conception of the poem, we can also relinquish what

Elizabeth Bishop called "the immodest demand. . . for complete comprehension." The best poems retain a mystery at their core that we will *never* fully understand, an experience ultimately beyond the grasp of the grasping mind. The poem that can be explained is not the true poem.

When I was in graduate school, deconstruction was in vogue, and literature professors and PhD students would often speak of "interrogating" a poem, seemingly unaware of or unbothered by the association of interrogation with torture. It was not enough to study or appreciate a poem, you had to *interrogate* it to prove that you were a tough-minded literary critic, and more importantly to show that you held the poem in your power, regarded it with suspicion, and could make it say what you wanted it to say, by violence if necessary. This way of reading, which still persists in academic settings, is antithetical to the appreciative mode; it is fundamentally aggressive and arises from our desire to control the messy, unpredictable flow of life, to impose fixity on flux.

The practice of appreciative attention can relax the grasping mind and our anxious need to control.

And this practice is refreshingly uncomplicated: we simply *attend to and savor* what we find most pleasing or compelling or resonant in the poem, what feels most alive, most lit up. It may be a line or a stanza; an image, a metaphor, a gesture; a surprising turn or stunning connection; a "lucid, inescapable rhythm," to use Wallace Stevens's arresting phrase; an upsurge of emotion, a profound insight, a compelling tone of voice; perhaps a single perfectly chosen, unexpectedly splendid word; or perhaps the whole arc of the poem, the journey it takes us on. Whatever it is that calls to us, the practice is to savor it, to linger, to let your appreciation deepen and expand and take you where it will. Reading poems in this way can help us slow down and stay present with what's right in front of us, on the page and in our lives.

When our orientation to the poem is appreciative rather than interpretive, when we make primary what we love rather than what we understand (or don't understand), the poem opens itself more fully to our gaze. And the more we see, the more the poem shows us. Just as a person will relax and come alive when they feel truly seen, poems begin to glow in the light of our appreciative attention. Iain McGilchrist in *The Master and His Emissary: The Divided Brain and the Making of the Western World* suggests that we experience works of art as being more like people than things. Works of art, especially those that unfold in time like poetry and music, possess a quality of aliveness, an organic self-coherence, that is subtle, fluid, complex, and responsive to our awareness.

We think the world out there, poetry included, is unaffected by and indifferent to the quality of our attention, but it isn't. When we look with love at the world, when we are in an appreciative mode of consciousness, we change the world we see. With the discovery of the "observer effect," quantum physics verified what poets and mystics have known for ages: that, as Wordsworth said, we "half create" what we perceive. We know intuitively how this works in the realm of emotion. If we move through the world in a state of anger, anger will find us. When we approach the world with a loving awareness, the world gives us more to love.

It is not so much *what* we see but *how* we see. As Baba Hari Dass said, "When a pickpocket meets a saint, all he sees are his pockets." (We might also say that when a saint meets a pickpocket, all he sees is his divine essence.) The same is true for poetry. When we attune to the spiritual dimension of poetry, we begin to see that poems are by their very nature spiritual.

In some mystical philosophies—Taoism is the prime example—the divine is conceived of not as a being but a process, a perpetual becoming, a ceaseless and mysterious generative flow rather than an unchanging supernatural entity. A contemporary expression of this idea comes from the Franciscan mystic Richard Rohr, for whom God is "a flow, an inner aliveness, a dynamism, moving forward and toward, and never a static Zeus figure sitting on a throne, who must be placated and feared." Poems can embody this ongoing aliveness, can be a conduit for it, because poems—great poems—issue from flow states themselves, from *inspiration*, from a kind of divine guidance. So when we enter the poem's flow—and appreciative attention helps us enter—we experience a current, or undercurrent, of this larger flow that is always all around us but which remains hidden and seemingly inaccessible. A poem is a particular manifestation of it, a particular immanence of this transcendent, generative power.

Even poems that are not spiritual in any obvious way can still convey a quality of sacredness if the poet was in a flow state when the poem came into form. The content of the poem—all that happens in it, all that can be pointed to—doesn't really matter. What matters is that the poem allows us to make contact with this creative flow, invites us to participate in it. When that happens, we get a taste of the sacred, we attune to it, we feel it. And that is why, or partly why, reading a great poem can be so transformative: it brings us into congruence with the truth of things and reminds us of our own true nature, our Buddha nature—open, untainted, alive to the moment, at peace with life's unfolding.

Though not typically understood as such, flow states in my view are intrinsically spiritual. They bring us to a kind of temporary enlightenment. In flow, we are released from all egoic constrictions, freed from grasping and aversion. The sense of separation falls away as we immerse ourselves wholeheartedly in whatever we're doing, whatever is arising in the present moment. Time slows down, or disappears altogether; the intuitive mind comes forward as the analytical mind recedes to its proper supportive role; we feel guided by something larger than ourselves that we can't control but can attune to and allow to move through us. Concentration is intense but also effortless, focused but also wide open. Self-consciousness falls away, and we feel the rightness of every spontaneous decision. There is no disruption between the flow of our awareness and the flow of life itself. It is a blessed state.

There are many extraordinary examples of sustained flow states in poetry. All 162 lines of Wordsworth's masterpiece "Tintern Abbey" came to him while walking in the Welsh moors; he merely wrote them down after returning. Rilke wrote much of his ecstatic *Duino Elegies* over the course of several days of continuous inspiration, in the grip of what he called "a boundless storm, a hurricane of the spirit." A. R. Ammons wrote an entire book-length poem, *Tape for the Turn of the Year,* on a roll of adding-machine tape run through a typewriter. He simply recorded what came to him each day, without premeditation or revision, trusting that he was making himself available "to the self not mine but ours," as he says in "Poetics." Which is another way of describing a flow state, a state of deep allowing in which the poet becomes a conduit for what Emerson called "the currents of the Universal Being." When asked about her creative process, Ruth Stone replied that she did not write her poems but received them. "Even as a child, I would hear a poem coming toward me from way off in the universe. I wouldn't hear it. I would feel it, and it would come right toward me. If I didn't catch it, if I didn't run in the house and write it down, it would go right through me and back into the universe." Not all poems come in this way—and of course much dedicated work precedes the creative burst—but I would argue all the best ones do.

Even a poem as brief as a haiku can arise from and bring us into contact with the pure flow of awareness. This one by Christopher Herold carries the fragrance of the sacred and reminds us of our untainted true nature:

> cherry petals
> a child adds a handful
> to the busker's cap

How wonderful to see the child, presumably after watching adults dropping money in the hat, gather up a handful of cherry petals to make an offering. And how innocently subversive is this substitution, how meaningless and valueless money seems compared to cherry petals, a true poetic currency. The moment delights in part because that creative, generous impulse is still alive in us. It may be buried beneath layers of habit and conditioning, but when we see it in a poem like this, we feel lit up inside. We know on some level that this is who we are and how we wish to be: childlike, unselfconscious, spontaneously responsive to life as it is.

We also delight in the poet's preserving this moment and rendering it so simply, succinctly, and beautifully, the unadorned, just this-ness of the poem itself. In response we offer our appreciative attention, our own cherry petals, and so the energetic frequency of gratitude and generosity is amplified as we appreciate the poet's appreciation of the child's appreciation of the busker's performance. Such appreciation, as I suggested in the introduction, is not only a beneficent mind state, a joy in and of itself, but a necessary precondition for reverence to arise.

~

As we practice appreciative attention with poetry, we may begin to practice it in our lives as well. We may begin to move through our world noticing more, savoring moments of unexpected delight and looking for beauty and goodness even in the most unlikely places, remembering that it's not *what* we see but *how* we see that matters most. "How hidden is the sacred," Danusha Laméris writes in "O Darkness," reminding us that the sacred is always both concealed and revealed, hidden in plain sight, as it were. Perhaps it is doubly hidden from us now, not because it is less present but because we have forgotten how to look for it, have lost the sense of wonder that allows us to see.

The Jewish theologian Abraham Joshua Heschel wrote,

> As civilization advances, the sense of wonder declines. Such decline is an alarming symptom of our state of mind. Mankind will not perish for want of information; but only for want of appreciation. The beginning of our happiness lies in the understanding that life without wonder is not worth living . . . Wonder or radical amazement . . . is therefore a prerequisite for an authentic awareness of that which is.

This decline in wonder also occurs in the development from childhood to adulthood, as the evolution of the individual recapitulates the evolution of the species. After flourishing in our first years of life, the sense of wonder gradually fades under the force of habit, repetition, and social conditioning. By the time we reach adulthood, we have absorbed, usually without conscious consideration, a materialist worldview founded on the assumption that whatever can't be measured doesn't exist or doesn't matter. And so the quality of wonder or "radical amazement" that Heschel identifies as central to who we are, and without which life is not worth living, is devalued, ignored, pushed to the margins. The conditions that make wonder more likely to arise are subsumed in our march toward greater efficiency and uniformity. We live in a disenchanted world.

And here is where poetry can help. We might think of poetry as an agent of re-enchantment. Wonder is at the heart of poetry, and I think that for most people, poets and readers alike, a significant relationship with poetry almost always begins in wonder. My own journey with poetry certainly did. When I started reading and writing poems in my late teens, the insufferable sameness and dullness of Nebraska was suddenly transformed as poetry taught me to actually look at the world rather than just have judgments about it. The endless cornfields I had always ignored, the rutted gravel roads, nameless creeks, nondescript grain silos, all so boring before, now seemed quietly beautiful, worth paying attention to. The landscape wasn't dramatic like the mountains of Colorado I was always pining for, but subtle. You had to *look for* what was beautiful, you had to go toward it, but it was there, waiting.

Suddenly everything repaid attention. I remember reading William Carlos Williams and walking through the dirt alleys in my neighborhood, marveling at the all things that had been banished to the bardo zone between usefulness and trash: old tools, broken furniture, rusting bikes, stacks of bricks, paint cans, dented hubcaps, etc. Such things now seemed both visually fascinating and possessed of a mysterious depth. They seemed wondrous. I wasn't aware of the Japanese aesthetic of *wabi-sabi* at the time, an aesthetic that values modest things marked by impermanence, imperfection, and melancholy, but I was intuitively aligned with those values. I loved weeds and weathered fence posts, old people, old houses—humble, discarded, neglected things. I had been around these things all my life but had never truly seen them. Poetry helped me see.

Or rather, poetry restored a way of seeing I had lost, a way of being alert for and attuned to wonder, open to its many unexpected manifestations. Connie Donleycott's haiku gives us a wonderful example:

crowd of umbrellas
a child opens his
face to the rain

Such a quietly stunning image, reminiscent of the great street photography of Henri Cartier-Bresson, Vivian Maier, Garry Winogrand, and others. And such a resonant contrast: the adults open their umbrellas to keep out the rain; the child opens his face to let it in. The poem doesn't insist on the significance of the scene, or any particular meaning we might find there, but it does lift up this moment from the rush of time and show it to us.

How we choose to see makes all the difference.

Biographical Notes

Elizabeth Alexander was born in 1962 in Harlem, New York, and grew up in Washington, DC. She earned degrees from Yale, Boston University, and the University of Pennsylvania, and taught at Yale for fifteen years, where she was chair of the African American Studies Department. She is also a founding member of Cave Canem, an organization dedicated to promoting African American poets and poetry, as well as a chancellor of the Academy of American Poets. The poet Clarence Major lauded Alexander's "instinct for turning her profound cultural vision into one that illuminates universal experience." Her poem "Praise Song for the Day," which she composed for Barack Obama's 2009 presidential inauguration and which appears in this anthology, does just that. At the time, Alexander was only the fourth poet to read at an American presidential inauguration, after Robert Frost in 1961, Maya Angelou in 1993 and Miller Williams in 1997. She is currently the president of the Andrew W. Mellon Foundation—the largest educational funder for arts, culture, and humanities in the United States. Her books of poetry include *Body of Life*, *American Sublime*, and *Crave Radiance: New and Selected Poems 1990–2010*. She has also published a memoir, *The Light of the World*, as well as two books of essays, *The Trayvon Generation* and *The Black Interior*. She lives in New York City.

A.R. Ammons was born in 1926 in rural North Carolina, near Whiteville, and grew up on a cotton and tobacco farm during the Great Depression. Ammons served on an escort destroyer as a sonar man, or "ping jockey," during the Second World War. After the war, he studied biology at Wake Forest University and literature at the University of California, Berkeley. He was vice president of a biological glass factory in New Jersey for several years before joining the faculty at Cornell University, where he taught until his death in 2001. Ammons twice won the National Book Award, for his *Collected Poems* in

1973 and for *Garbage* in 1993, a book-length poem about the transfiguration of matter into spirit, spirit into matter, or "stone into wind, wind into stone," as he put it. Ammons extended the Emersonian tradition, which he recast through a scientific understanding of natural processes, but was also strongly influenced by Taoist thought. In his most famous poem, "Corsons Inlet," Ammons enacts "the overall wandering of mirroring mind," a stance toward natural processes that ultimately derives from ancient Chinese poetry and philosophy. When asked whom he writes for, Ammons said, "I really don't write to an audience. I never imagined an audience. I imagine other lonely people such as myself. I don't know who they are or where they are, and I don't care. But those are the people whom I want to reach."

Ellen Bass was born in 1947 and grew up in Margate City, New Jersey. She studied with Anne Sexton at Boston University and credits Sexton with rescuing her from the critical discouragement she received from other teachers there. In addition to her books of poetry—*Mules of Love*, *The Human Line*, *Like a Beggar*, and *Indigo*—Bass co-edited with Florence Howe the groundbreaking anthology of feminist poetry *No More Masks!* She has also coauthored with Laura Davis the best-selling nonfiction book *The Courage to Heal: A Guide for Women Survivors of Child Sexual Abuse* and, with Kate Kaufman, *Free Your Mind: The Book for Gay, Lesbian and Bisexual Youth*. The influence of Buddhist thought is clear in Bass's poetry. Responding to the question of feeling exposed in her poems, Bass said in an interview that it's not in her choice of subjects that she feels exposed but in revealing how her mind works; "That's where I think the risk is. And maybe that's why people often feel so scared when they share their poetry—because you're exposing what it's like to be in your mind. That's intimate. I think that's the intimacy of poetry." She lives in Santa Cruz, California, where she teaches private in-person and online workshops. She is also on the faculty of the low-residency MFA program at Pacific University.

Prolific poet, novelist, essayist, farmer, and ecological activist, **Wendell Berry** was born in 1934 in Henry County, Kentucky, where the families of both of his parents had farmed for at least five generations. Berry earned a BA and an MA in English at the University of Kentucky before attending Stanford University's creative writing program as a Wallace Stegner Fellow. After several years traveling in Europe on a Guggenheim Fellowship and then teaching in New York City, Berry turned away from an academic career and in 1965 moved with his wife and two children to Lane's Landing, a twelve-acre farm on the western bank of the Kentucky River that eventually became a homestead of over one hundred acres. He has lived and farmed there ever since, while also teaching at the University of Kentucky. Both his writing and his ecological activism are deeply rooted in a sense of place and respect for the land. His many books include *The Unsettling of America: Culture and Agriculture*, *The Peace of Wild Things*, *A Place on Earth*, *A Small Porch: Sabbath Poems 2014 and 2015*, *The Gift of Good Land: Further Essays Cultural and Agricultural*, and *Bringing It to the Table: On Farming and Food* (with Michael Pollan). Speaking of the importance of community and neighborliness, Berry has said, "We really have to turn against the selfishness of the individualism that sees everybody as a competitor of everybody else. When we see how destructive that is, and we turn against it, then we have our life's work." He lives in Kentucky.

Elizabeth Bishop was born in 1911 in Worcester, Massachusetts. Her father died when she was eight months old, and her mother, who had suffered serious mental illness for many years, had to be permanently institutionalized when Bishop was just five, a traumatic experience Bishop wrote about in her short story "The Village." She lived for several years with her paternal grandparents, where she suffered emotional neglect and sexual abuse. While attending Vassar College, Bishop met Marianne Moore, and their friendship strongly influenced the young poet's early writing, just as Robert Lowell would influence her later work. Bishop lived in Boston, Key West, and New York City, but spent much of her adult life in Brazil with her partner, the architect Lota de Macedo Soares, who later committed suicide in New York City. Bishop herself struggled with depression and alcoholism for many years. She prized accuracy of observation in her poetry—she was also a fine watercolorist—and her poems exhibit a remarkable degree of mindfulness. In a letter to her biographer Anne Stevenson, Bishop said, "What one seems to want in art, in experiencing it, is the same thing that is necessary for its creation, a self-forgetful, perfectly useless concentration." She won the Pulitzer Prize in 1956 and the National Book Award in 1970. She died in 1979.

John Brandi was born in 1943, in Los Angeles, California. He studied art and anthropology at California State University, Northridge. After graduating in 1965, he spent two years as a Peace Corps volunteer in Ecuador working with Quechua farmers in their struggle for land rights. A lifelong "open roader," Brandi traveled extensively in India, China, Cuba, Vietnam, South American, the Himalayas, the Arctic, and the wilds of North American. He settled in New Mexico, where he built a hand-hewn cabin in the northern mountains and founded Tooth of Time Books, a small press devoted to poetry. For many years he taught in the Poetry-in-the-Schools programs throughout the western US and Alaska. A painter as well as a poet, Brandi has published travel books as well as hand-colored broadsides and limited-edition letterpress books. But he is best known as a haiku poet. In his introduction to *The Unswept Path: Contemporary American Haiku*, Brandi said, "We write poems to stay alive, to see where we've been, to give clearing for the next step. A deep surprise, a gong-rattling clonk, a giddy bafflement, a quiet revelation of the mysterious in the everyday: these zaps of primal, uninhibited delight are the seeds of haiku." His many books include *The Great Unrest*, *The Way to Thorong La*, and *Luminous Uplift: Landscape & Memory*. He lives in New Mexico.

John Brehm was born in Lincoln, Nebraska, in 1955. He received a BA in English from the University of Nebraska and an MFA in poetry from Cornell University, where he studied with A. R. Ammons. He has taught at Cornell, Emerson College, the University of Nebraska, Portland State University, Mountain Writers Workshop in Portland, Oregon, and the Lighthouse Writers Workshop in Denver,

Colorado. He offers a monthly Poetry as Spiritual Practice gathering and leads mindfulness retreats with his wife, Feldenkrais teacher Alice Boyd. Brehm is the author of four books of poetry: *Sea of Faith*, *Help Is on the Way*, *No Day at the Beach*, and *Dharma Talk*, as well as a book of essays, *The Dharma of Poetry: How Poems Can Deepen Your Spiritual Practice and Open You to Joy*. He is also the editor of *The Poetry of Impermanence, Mindfulness, and Joy* and the associate editor of *The Oxford Book of American Poetry*. He lives in Portland, Oregon.

Raymond Carver was born in 1938 in the logging town of Clatskanie, Oregon, and grew up in Yakima, Washington. He was married and the father of two children before he was twenty and worked variously as a delivery man, janitor, gas-station attendant, apartment-complex manager, and sawmill laborer. He attended Chico State University, where he studied with John Gardner, and earned his BA from Humboldt State College in 1963. Carver was accepted into the acclaimed Iowa Writers' Workshop but left before earning a degree. He went on to teach at the University of California at Santa Cruz, the

University of California at Berkeley, the University of Texas at El Paso, and Syracuse University. Carver struggled with alcoholism for much of his life and was hospitalized three times in the mid-1970s. With the help of Alcoholics Anonymous, he stopped drinking in 1977 and began what he referred to as his "second life," including a late happy marriage to the poet Tess Gallagher. Discussing subject matter in poetry and fiction, Carver said, "It's possible, in a poem or short story, to write about commonplace things and objects using commonplace but precise language, and to endow those things—a chair, a window curtain, a fork, a stone, a woman's earring—with immense, even startling power." Tess Gallagher said that for Carver, "poetry was a spiritual necessity." His books of poems include *Ultramarine*, *Where Water Comes Together with Other Water*, *A New Path to the Waterfall*, and *All of Us: Collected Poems*. He died in 1988.

Haiku poet **Yu Chang** was born in 1938 in mainland China and grew up in Taiwan. After moving to the United States, he earned graduate degrees at the University of Wisconsin and Syracuse University and taught for many years at Union College in Schenectady, New York, where he is now professor emeritus of electrical engineering. His work has won the Museum of Haiku Literature Award in *Frogpond* (1998, 2009) and the Haiku Society of America's Harold G. Henderson Award (1999). His books include *seeds* and *Small Things Make Me Laugh*. He was a founding member of the Route 9 Haiku Group and has been editor of its journal, *Upstate Dim Sum*, since 2001. Of his book *seeds*, Peggy Willis Lyles observed, "Whether offering a moment's self-revelation or calling attention to a commonplace scene, Yu Chang's haiku and *senryu* establish connections that move straight to the heart." He lives in Schenectady, New York.

Born in 1947, **Margaret Chula** grew up on her grandparents' tobacco farm on the banks of the Connecticut River, where she explored eighty acres of woods and meadows. In her thirties, she traveled around the world with her husband and then settled in Kyoto for twelve years, teaching English and creative writing at Kyoto Seika University and other schools. There, she became friends with Edith Shiffert and began writing haiku after discovering R. H. Blyth's translations of the great Japanese haiku masters. She has published twelve collections of poetry, including *Grinding My Ink*, which received the Haiku Society of America Book Award; *One Leaf Detaches*, a 2019 Touchstone Distinguished Book Award winner; and *Firefly Lanterns: Twelve Years in Kyoto*, a book of *haibun* (mixed prose and haiku). She served for five years as president of the Tanka Society of America and currently sits on the advisory board of the Center for Japanese Studies at Portland State University. Asked in an interview what she most enjoys about haiku, Chula said, "I enjoy the simplicity and openness of haiku—how two seemingly unrelated images come together to create an emotional resonance. I enjoy how haiku allow each of us to fill in the spaces with our own experience. Writing haiku centers me in the present, much like the tea ceremony expression *ichi go, ichi e* (one time, one encounter). Treasure the moment, the people you are with. This experience will never happen again." She lives in Portland, Oregon.

Lucille Clifton was born in 1936 in DePew, New York, and grew up in Buffalo. She attended Howard University before transferring to the State University of New York, Fredonia. Clifton's poetic career took off when her friend Ishmael Reed shared her poems with Langston Hughes, who included her in his highly influential anthology *The Poetry of the Negro*. Her first book of poems, *Good Times* (1969), was rated one of the best books of the year by the *New York Times* and was followed by *Good News About the Earth* in 1972 and *An Ordinary Woman* in 1974. In 1987, Clifton was the first author to have two books of poetry chosen as finalists for the Pulitzer Prize in the same year: *Good Woman: Poems and a Memoir, 1969–1980* and *Next: New Poems*. She served as the state of Maryland's poet laureate from 1974 until 1985 and won the National Book Award for *Blessing the Boats: New and Selected Poems, 1988–2000*. She was also awarded the Ruth Lilly Prize from the Poetry Foundation and the Frost Medal from the Poetry Society of America. In addition to her many poetry collections, she has written numerous children's books. Clifton was a Distinguished Professor of Humanities at St. Mary's

College of Maryland and a chancellor of the Academy of American Poets. In her obituary for the *New Yorker*, Elizabeth Alexander observed that Clifton's style "was as understated as the lowercase type of her poems, a quiet, even woman's voice telling sometimes terrible truths. Like psalms, koans, and old folks' proverbs, Clifton's poems invite meditation and return." She struggled with health issues for much of her life, receiving a kidney transplant and battling several bouts of cancer, and died in 2010 at the age of seventy-three.

David Cobb was born in 1926 in Harrow, England. He had a distinguished career in teaching languages and literature, initially in the United Kingdom, then in Germany and Thailand. Beginning in 1968, he was an adviser or author for over one hundred schoolbooks used worldwide. He launched the British Haiku Society in 1990 and served as its president from 1997 to 2002. His book *The Consensus* was used worldwide as a guide to haiku writing and was republished as *English Haiku: A Composite View*. Cobb also pioneered English-language *haibun*, a mix of prose and haiku. His books of original poetry include *Anchorage: Selected Haiku, 1991–2013*, *Spitting Pips*, and *Marching with Tulips*. He also edited several acclaimed anthologies, including *Haiku: The British Museum*, *Haiku: The Poetry of Nature*, and *Euro-Haiku: A Bilingual Anthology*. Describing Cobb's work, the American critic Michael McClintock said, "Gentle, melancholy, ruminative aspects make his poems distinctive among contemporary English-language haiku." He died in Essex, England, in 2020.

Billy Collins was born in 1941 in New York City and grew up in Queens and White Plains, New York. He received a BA in English from the College of the Holy Cross in 1963 and an MA and PhD in romantic poetry from the University of California, Riverside. Collins served two terms as the United States poet laureate (2001–3) and was New York State poet laureate from 2004 to 2006. He is a regular guest on National Public Radio programs, including Garrison Keillor's *Writer's Almanac*. Collins's books include *The Trouble with Poetry*, *Whale Day*, *Musical Tables*, *The Rain in Portugal*, and *Aimless Love: New and Selected Poems*.

His poems are notable for their humor, accessibility, and charm; his meditations on daily life, or on such subjects as history, art, and poetry itself, often take unexpected, whimsical turns. The critic John Taylor wrote of Collins that "rarely has anyone written poems that appear so transparent on the surface yet become so ambiguous, thought-provoking, or simply wise once the reader has peered into the depths." Collins lives in Sommers, New York.

Carl Dennis was born in St. Louis, Missouri, in 1939. After studying at Oberlin College and the University of Chicago, he received a BA from the University of Minnesota and a PhD in English literature from the University of California, Berkeley. He taught for many years at the State University of New York at Buffalo. In quietly meditative and philosophical poems, Dennis explores the intricacies of daily life and the perennial themes of the human predicament. In an interview he observed, "When I'm moved by a poem, I feel that an intractable human problem has been treated fully and sympathetically. When poetry works, it offers evidence that the reader is not alone, that someone else has felt and thought what the reader has felt. When this happens poetry proves itself the most intimate kind of writing." Dennis has published fourteen books of poetry, including *Practical Gods*, for which he won the Pulitzer Prize; *Callings*; *Another Reason*; *Night School*; and *Earthborn*, as well as a book of essays, *Poetry as Persuasion*. He lives in Buffalo, New York.

Patricia Donegan was born in 1925 in Chicago. She served on the faculty of East-West Poetics at Naropa University under Allen Ginsberg and Chögyam Trungpa Rinpoche, was a student of haiku master Seishi Yamaguchi, and was a Fulbright scholar to Japan. Donegan was a poetry editor for *Kyoto Journal* and a longtime member of the Haiku Society of America. Her anthologies and translations include *Love Haiku: Japanese Poems of Yearning*; *Passion & Remembrance*, co-translated with Yoshie Ishibashi; *Haiku Mind: 108 Poems to Cultivate Awareness and Open Your Heart*; *Haiku: Asian Arts for Creative Kids*; and *Chiyo-ni Woman Haiku Master*, co-translated with Yoshie Ishibashi. Her poetry collections include *Hot Haiku*, *Bone Poems*,

Without Warning, and *Heralding the Milk Light*. Her books on haiku have combined scholarship and insight in reaching young and old to inspire and sustain a lifelong interest in haiku poetry, in both Japanese and English. In her essay "An Antidote to Speed," Donegan writes that "haiku brings us the birth and death of each moment. Everything is stripped away to its naked state. No high-tech speed, but slowly and naturally we discover what is simply here, as in meditation: our aging bodies, the afternoon light on the bed sheets, the sound of a siren in the distance—whatever is contained in this moment, without adornment." She died in 2022.

Connie Donleycott was born in 1953 in Aberdeen, Washington. She received her associate arts degree from Olympia College in Bremerton, Washington, in 1973. From there she attended ITT Peterson's School of Business in Seattle and received her legal secretarial degree. From 1974 to 1980, she worked at the Kitsap County Courthouse in Management & Budget. In both 2001 and 2003, Donleycott received the Readers' Choice–Valentine Award

Poem of the Year from the *Heron's Nest* haiku journal. In 2004, her haiku "bases loaded . . . / the peanut vendor / throws another strike" was chosen to be one of the "Facts & Fictions" Poetry on Busses placards in the Seattle Metro area. One of her haiku has been engraved on a river boulder at the Kati Kati Haiku Pathway Natural reserve in Kati Kati, New Zealand. She lives in Bremerton, Washington.

Emily Fragos was born in 1949 in Mount Vernon, New York. She received a BA from Syracuse University, an MA from La Sorbonne in Paris, and an MFA from Columbia University. Her books of poetry include *Little Savage*, *Saint Torch*, *Unrest*, and *Hostage: New and Selected Poems*. She has also edited six best-selling anthologies for the Everyman's Pocket Library: *The Letters of Emily Dickinson*, *Music's Spell*, *The Dance*, *The Great Cat*, *Art & Artists*, and *Gratitude*. Fragos currently teaches at New York University and Columbia University. She has long volunteered to teach poetry workshops for the disabled and elderly at nursing and rehabilitation centers in Westchester, New York. In 2014 she received an Arts & Letters Award in Literature from the American Academy of Arts and Letters. In the *Boston Review*, Marie Ponsot observed, "Fragos is a thin-skinned, tough-minded poet of this world. Her sensual sensibility is unrestrained by conventional perceptual grids. Her poems take us by surprise. . . . We are enlarged by her resonant verbal imagination." Fragos lives in New York City.

Robert Frost was born in San Francisco in 1874 but lived most of his life in rural New England. Though he cultivated a public persona of the plain-speaking farmer-poet—and in fact never finished a college degree—Frost was a highly sophisticated artist. He read widely in the Greek and Latin classics in their original languages and was perhaps the most skillful formalist of the twentieth century. Frost's personal life was marked by impermanence and tragedy. His father, a newspaperman, died of tuberculosis when Frost was eleven, leaving the family destitute; his mother, whose Swedenborgian mysticism was a major influence on her son, died of cancer in 1900. His younger sister Jeanie had to be committed to a mental hospital in 1920, and Frost himself feared at times for his own sanity. Mental illness ran in his family—his daughter Irma also had to be committed to a mental hospital, and his son Carol committed suicide. Another son died of cholera at age eight, and two of his daughters also died young: Elinor Bettina, just three days after her birth, and Marjorie of puerperal fever after giving birth at twenty-nine. Of the poetic process, Frost said, "All I would keep for myself is the freedom of my material—the condition of body and mind now and then to summon aptly from the vast chaos of all I have lived through." He was awarded the Pulitzer Prize four times and attained a popularity unprecedented and unsurpassed among American poets. He read his poem "The Gift Outright" at the inauguration of President John F. Kennedy in 1961. He died in 1963.

Born in 1949 in Smiths Falls, Ontario, Canada, **LeRoy Gorman** grew up on a farm near Merrickville, Ontario. He graduated from Carleton University and then Queen's University, before beginning a nearly forty-year teaching career, first with the Ontario Ministry of Correctional Services, and later with the Algonquin and Lakeshore Catholic District School Board in Ontario. Gorman's haiku, *haikai* (a more playful and often humorous subtype of haiku), and other forms of poetry have appeared in publications and exhibitions worldwide. He is the author of two dozen poetry books and chapbooks, including *Gathering Light*, *Heart's Garden*, *seasons on the run*, *flurries*, and *fast enough to leave this world*. From 1995 to 2017 he served as editor of Haiku Canada Publications (*Haiku Canada Newsletter* 1995–2006, *Haiku Canada Review* 2007–17). For his significant contributions, he was recognized as a life member of Haiku Canada. In announcing his appointment as honorary curator of the American Haiku Archives (2012–13), Michael Dylan Welch observed that Gorman's poetry "consistently shows admirable creativity, courage, and range, embracing both traditional and visual/minimalist approaches to haiku and related genres of poetry." Since 1998, he has published poetry leaflets and postcards under his PawEpress imprint. He lives in Napanee, Ontario.

Poet, playwright, memoirist, musician, and children's book author **Joy Harjo** was born in 1951 in Tulsa, Oklahoma. Her father, Allen W. Foster, was a member of the Muscogee (Creek) Nation, and her mother, Wynema Baker Foster, was of mixed Cherokee and European-American ancestry. Harjo herself is a member of the Muscogee (Creek) Nation. She attended high school at the Institute of American Indian Arts, completed her undergraduate degree at the University of New Mexico, and earned an MFA at the University of Iowa. She has taught at the Institute of American Indian Arts, Arizona State University, the University of New Mexico, the University of California at Los Angeles, and several other colleges and universities. She served as the United States poet laureate from 2019 to 2022, the first Native American to hold that honor. Her many books include *Weaving Sundown in a Scarlet Light*, *Catching the Light*, *Poet Warrior*, *Conflict Resolution for Holy Beings*, *Crazy Brave*, and *How We Became Human: New and Selected Poems 1975–2002*. Harjo is also the executive editor of the anthology *When the Light of the World Was Subdued, Our Songs Came Through: A Norton Anthology of Native Nations Poetry* and the editor of

Living Nations, Living Words: An Anthology of First Peoples Poetry. Harjo has described poetry as "the voice of what can't be spoken, the mode of truth-telling when meaning needs to rise above or skim below everyday language in shapes not discernible by the ordinary mind. . . . Poetry is prophetic by nature and not bound by time. Because of these qualities, poetry carries grief, heartache, ecstasy, celebration, despair, or searing truth more directly than any other literary art form. It is ceremonial in nature. . . Without poetry, we lose our way." She lives in Tulsa, Oklahoma.

Robert Hayden was born in 1913 in Detroit, Michigan, and grew up in the gritty Detroit neighborhood of Paradise Valley. His parents separated before his birth, and he was taken in by a foster family next door. His foster parents frequently fought, and Hayden himself was subject to beatings. Extremely nearsighted, unathletic, and often depressed, Hayden did not participate in sports or fit in socially, taking refuge in literature instead. He attended Detroit City College (now Wayne State University) but left in 1936 during the Great Depression, one credit short of finishing his degree, to join the Works Progress Administration's Federal Writers' Project, researching Black history and folk culture. Hayden went on to earn an MA in English literature at the University of Michigan, where he studied under W. H. Auden. Though he was raised Baptist, he embraced the Bahá'í Faith in the early 1940s and became one of the best-known Bahá'í poets. Hayden taught at Fisk University for many years, as well as at the University of Michigan. He eventually became the first African American to be appointed as consultant in poetry to the Library of Congress, a position now known as the United States poet laureate. Discussing his admiration for Frederick Douglass, Hayden emphasized the "universality in his outlook, and some sense of the basic unity, the basic oneness of mankind," which Hayden identified as a cardinal principle of his own Bahá'í Faith. His collections of poetry include *Heart-Shape in the Dust*; *Figure of Time*; *A Ballad of Remembrance*, which won the grand prize at the First World Festival of Negro Arts in Dakar, Senegal; *The Night-Blooming Cereus*; *Angle of Ascent: New and Selected Poems*; and *American Journal*. He died in 1966.

Nobel Laureate **Seamus Heaney** was born in 1939, at the family farmhouse in County Derry, Northern Ireland, the eldest of nine children. His father was a small farmer and cattle dealer, and Heaney's poetry owes much of its sensuous richness to his early life on the farm. He studied English at Queen's University in Belfast and went on to teach at the University of California at Berkeley, Harvard University, Oxford University, and several other colleges. His many books of poetry, prose, translations, and plays include *Field Work*, *Station Island*, *Door into the Dark*, *The Spirit Level*, *Burial at Thebes*, and *The Redress of Poetry*. He was awarded the Nobel Prize in Literature 1995 "for works of lyrical beauty and ethical depth, which exalt everyday miracles and the living past." In an interview with the *Guardian*, Heaney said, "The experiment of poetry, as far as I am concerned, happens when the poem carries you beyond where you could have reasonably expected to go. The image I have is from the old cartoons: Donald Duck or Mickey Mouse coming hell-for-leather to the edge of a cliff, skidding to a stop but unable to halt, and shooting out over the edge. A good poem is the same, it

goes that bit further and leaves you walking on air."
Heaney died in 2013.

Christopher Herold was born in 1948 in Suffern, New York, and grew up in the San Francisco Bay Area. Since 1998, he has lived in Port Townsend, Washington. In addition to being an award-winning haiku poet, Herold is a percussionist who has performed and/or recorded with John Lee Hooker, T-Bone Walker, Jerry Garcia, Mike Bloomfield, and many others. Herold was a student of Shunryu Suzuki Roshi at the Tassajara Zen Mountain Center and is a lay Buddhist monk in the Sōtō tradition. He has taught haiku at all levels from grade school to adult workshops. In 1999, he cofounded the haiku journal the *Heron's Nest*, for which he was managing editor until 2008. Herold's books include *Inside Out*, *In Other Words*, *Coincidence*, *Voices of Stone*, *A Path in the Garden* (winner of a Haiku Society of America Merit Book Award), and *In the Margins of the Sea*. Asked about what mindset he likes to be in when writing haiku, Herold replied, "Actually, I'd prefer to be free of any mindset. It's important to me to be aware of and to resist preconditioned responses so that they don't interfere with my recognizing the essence of an experience. In other words, I want to get out of the way so that the experience can materialize in words with as little manipulation as possible. The best way I've found to facilitate this is to clear my mind of 'rules' and focus as fully as I can on conjuring up the moment that inspired me. Then I wait patiently. More often than not, words eventually surface of themselves."

Poet, translator, and essayist **David Hinton** was born in 1954 in Salt Lake City, Utah. He did his undergraduate work at the University of Utah and received an MFA in poetry from Cornell University. He went on to study Chinese at Cornell and in Taiwan, and has taught at Columbia University and Freie Universität in Berlin. Hinton's translations from Chinese include *Classical Chinese Poetry: An Anthology*; *The Mountain Poems of Hsieh Ling-yun*; *The Analects of Confucius*; *Chuang Tzu: Inner Chapters*; *The Selected Poems of Li Po*; and *The Selected Poems of Tu Fu*. He is also the author of several prose works: *The Way of Ch'an: Essential Texts* of the Original Tradition; *Wild Mind, Wild Earth: Our Place in the Sixth Extinction*; *The Wilds of Poetry: Adventures in Mind and Landscape*; and *Hunger Mountain: A Field Guide to Mind and Landscape*. He is the author of two books of poems: *Fossil Sky* and *Desert*. Discussing the importance of awe and wonder in an interview, Hinton said, "In a sense, each time we look at a mountain and feel awe, it deconstructs Western metaphysics a bit, because it shows that we're not isolated; we're in communication with the world. And now, more and more in this age of vast ecological destruction, people are finding that they 'feel' it, that they grieve over it." In 2014, he was awarded the Thornton Wilder Prize for Translation by the American Academy of Arts and Letters. He lives in Vermont with his wife, the poet Jody Gladding.

A Chickasaw poet, novelist, essayist, and environmentalist, **Linda Hogan** was born in 1947 in Denver, Colorado. She earned an undergraduate degree from the University of Colorado, Colorado Springs, and an MA in English and creative writing from the University of Colorado, Boulder. Her books of poems include *Calling Myself Home*; *Daughters, I Love You*; *Seeing Through the Sun*, which won the American Book Award from the Before Columbus Foundation; *The Book of Medicines*, a National Book Critics Circle Award finalist; and *Dark. Sweet.: New and Selected Poems*. She has also written widely on ecological and Native American issues in such prose collections as *Dwellings: A Spiritual History of the Living World*, *The Woman Who Watches Over the World: A Native Memoir*, and *The Radiant Lives of Animals*. In an interview, Hogan spoke about the importance of animals in her life and writing: "I don't know if we need animals to keep us close to the divine, but I need wilderness, the sunrise every morning, all the possible life around me, to be a whole human, with joy inside. I think that must be the divine." Hogan has taught at the University of Colorado, at the Indigenous Education Institute, and at the Indian Arts Institute in Santa Fe. She also volunteered for six years at Birds of Prey Rehabilitation Center in Colorado Springs. Hogan has been a speaker at the United Nations Forum and was a plenary speaker at the Environmental Literature Conference in Turkey in 2009. She lives in Tishomingo, Oklahoma.

Andrea Hollander (formerly Andrea Hollander Budy) was born in Berlin, Germany, in 1947 to American parents, and raised in Colorado, Texas, New York, and New Jersey. She was educated at Boston University and the University of Colorado. For many years she lived in relative isolation on fifty-two wooded acres in the Ozark Mountains of Arkansas, having little contact with other writers and the larger literary world. She published her first book, *House Without a Dreamer*, in 1993 at the age of forty-six. Her other published volumes include *Woman in the Painting*, *The Other Life*, *Landscape with Female Figure: New and Selected Poems*, and *And Now, Nowhere But Here*. She was writer-in-residence for twenty-two years at Lyon College and currently lives in Portland, Oregon. Of learning the craft of poetry, Hollander has written, "I do not have a degree in creative writing. I learned and continue to learn the craft of writing by studying powerful poems by others. If each such poem is a trick performed by a master magician, I, an aspiring or apprentice magician, must try to figure out how the magic works, and—because no master magician gives away secrets—I must discern this completely on my own."

Christopher Howell was born in 1945 in Portland, Oregon. He served as journalist for the U.S. Navy during the Vietnam War. After the war, he earned a BS from Oregon State University, an MA from Portland State University, and an MFA from the University of Massachusetts, Amherst. Since 1972, Howell has been the director and principal editor for Lynx House Press, which awards the Blue Lynx Prize for Poetry. Howell is also editor of Willow Springs Books and is on the faculty of the MFA program in creative writing at Eastern Washington University. His daughter, Emma Howell, was an aspiring poet and student at Oberlin College who died at age twenty in June 2001. Her family published her poems posthumously in a volume titled *Slim Night of Recognition*. In an interview, Howell spoke about grief in his poetry: "There is a phrase in Latin, *lacrimae rerum*, 'the tears of things'. I think of the sadness in my work in those terms, that it is an acknowledgment of some fundamental mortal sadness essential to life, and that it is only a micron from joy. Grief, it seems to me, has more specific sources and is more personal. But it is also a blessing, since it allows the one who grieves to affirm, again, that powerful affection for what has been lost. And right next to grief, I think, only a whisper away, is celebration." Howell lives in Spokane, Washington.

Born in 1968 in Philadelphia, Pennsylvania, **Major Jackson** is the author of six collections of poetry, including *Razzle Dazzle: New & Selected Poems*, *The Absurd Man*, *Holding Company*, *Hoops*, and *Leaving Saturn*, which won the 2000 Cave Canem Poetry Prize and was a finalist for a National Book Critics Award Circle. He has also edited several anthologies: *Best American Poetry 2019*, *Renga for Obama*, and the Library of America's *Countee Cullen: Collected Poems*. Jackson earned degrees from Temple University and the University of Oregon and has taught at the University of Vermont at Bennington, New York University, and Vanderbilt University, where he currently teaches. He is the poetry editor of the *Harvard Review* and hosts the podcast *The Slowdown*. In an interview, Jackson said that he sees poetry as "an opportunity to slow our day down, be reflective, and contemplate our space in the world and how the world affects us. That practice of putting down language in meticulous fashion, as a mode of inquiry, to discover how we feel and how we respond to the world . . . I believe has a profound psychic, psychological, and physiological effect. It's a way to take care of ourselves." Jackson lives in Nashville, Tennessee.

Robinson Jeffers was born in 1887 in Allegheny, Pennsylvania, a town which is now part of Pittsburgh. His father, a minister and scholar of ancient languages and biblical history, oversaw his education. Jeffers began studying Greek at age five and by twelve was fluent in French and German. He graduated from Occidental College at eighteen and went on to study literature and, later, medicine at the University of Southern California and forestry at the University of Washington. He built a stone cottage and a forty-foot tower on the cliff above Carmel Bay and took inspiration from the awesome beauty of the California coast, where many of his poems are set. Jeffers was a fierce critic of modern Western civilization, particularly its destructive relationship to the natural world, its addiction to comfort, and its endless wars. In many of his poems and prose writings, he prefigures contemporary ecological perspectives, and once said, "I believe the universe is one being, all its parts are different expressions of the same energy, and they are all in communication with each other, influencing each other, therefore parts of one organic whole. . . . The whole is in all its parts so beautiful . . . that I am compelled to love it, and to think of it as divine." Jeffers achieved a remarkable degree of fame for an American poet, appearing on the cover of *Time* magazine in 1932. But he was widely criticized for his opposition to American involvement in the Second World War, and public opinion largely turned against him and his uncompromising devotion to nature over man. "The human race will cease after a while," he said, "but the great splendors of nature will go on." Jeffers died in 1962.

Galway Kinnell was born in 1927 in Providence, Rhode Island. He graduated from Princeton University in 1948, where he was classmates with W. S. Merwin. After serving in the United States Navy, Kinnell spent several years traveling, including extensive tours of Europe and the Middle East, especially Iran and France. After returning to the States, he joined CORE (Congress of Racial Equality) as a field worker and spent much of the 1960s involved in the civil rights movement. He was arrested while participating in a workplace integration in Louisiana. Kinnell's social and antiwar activism informed two of his most celebrated collections, *Body Rags* and *The Book of Nightmares*. He won both the Pulitzer Prize and the National Book Award for his *Selected Poems*. He also published translations of works by Yves Bonnefoy, Yvan Goll, François Villon, and Rainer Maria Rilke. About his work, Liz Rosenberg wrote in the *Boston Globe* that "Kinnell is a poet of the rarest ability, the kind who comes once or twice in a generation, who can flesh out music, raise the spirits and break the heart." Kinnell taught at New York

University for many years and served as the poet laureate of Vermont. He died in 2014.

Yusef Komunyakaa was born in 1947 in Bogalusa, Louisiana. He served in the United States Army during the Vietnam War as a correspondent and as managing editor of the *Southern Cross*. He was a awarded a Bronze Star for his service, and his collection *Dien Cai Dau* has been hailed as among the best books about the Vietnam War. He won the Pulitzer Prize for *Neon Vernacular: New & Selected Poems*. His other books include *Pleasure Dome: New and Collected Poems*, *Everyday Mojo Songs of Earth: New and Selected Poems, 2001–2021*, and *Condition Red: Essays, Interviews, and Commentaries*. Strongly influenced by jazz, especially African American jazz musicians of the 1950s and 60s, Komunyakaa has said, "Jazz has space, and space equals freedom, a place where the wheels of imagination can turn and a certain kind of meditation can take place." Komunyakaa is currently professor of English at New York University, where he teaches poetry and creative writing.

Greg Kosmicki was born in 1949 in Alliance, Nebraska. He received a BA and an MA in English from the University of Nebraska, Lincoln. In 1998 he founded the Backwaters Press, now an imprint of the University of Nebraska Press. Kosmicki has published fourteen books and chapbooks, including *We Eat the Earth*; *As Good Here as it Gets Anywhere*, which was a 2017 finalist for the High Plains Book Award; *Some Hero of the Past*; and *We Have Always Been Coming to This Morning*. He has been awarded two Artist's Fellowships by the Nebraska Arts Council for his poetry. For twenty-five years he worked in social services for the State of Nebraska. Asked what sparks poetry for him, Kosmicki said, "My writing is usually triggered by or suggested by interactions with people or with other creatures. If I pay attention—and I think that nearly a hundred percent of writing is paying attention—something about any interaction with another living being will give me a slightly different angle of view which presents an entryway into writing." He lives in Omaha, Nebraska.

Danusha Laméris was born in 1971 in Cambridge, Massachusetts, to a Dutch father and a Caribbean mother from the island of Barbados. She grew up in Mill Valley and Berkeley, California, and graduated from the University of California at Santa Cruz with a BA in studio art. She is the author of two books of poems: *The Moons of August* and *Bonfire Opera*. In an interview, Laméris said, "I see myself as someone who lost my innocence early, who faced the death of a child, my brother's suicide, a difficult childhood. Now I put my faith in what is unfinished, off-center, a kind of psycho-spiritual expression of *wabi-sabi*, the Japanese aesthetic concept of admiring that which is worn-in, imperfect, altered by time. If we can praise what is flawed and tattered and half-done, we can praise so many things." The poet laureate of Santa Cruz from 2018 to 2020, she teaches in Pacific University's low-residency MFA program and lives in Santa Cruz, California.

Philip Larkin was born in 1922 in Coventry, Warwickshire, England. After graduating from Oxford University, Larkin became librarian at the University of Hull in Yorkshire in 1955, where he worked for the rest of his life. In addition to the four books of poetry—*The North Ship*, *The Less Deceived*, *High Windows*, and *The Whitsun Weddings*—Larkin published a collection of essays, *All What Jazz*, drawn from his work as a jazz critic for the *Daily Telegraph*, and a book of miscellaneous essays, *Required Writing*, as well as two novels, *Jill* and *A Girl in Winter*. He also edited the *Oxford Book of Twentieth-Century English Verse*. Larkin was a decidedly anti-Romantic poet, often glum, often bitingly witty, who famously said, "Deprivation is for me what daffodils were to Wordsworth." He was close friends with the novelist Kingsley Amis, and the protagonist of Amis's *Lucky Jim* is based on Larkin. He was offered, but refused, the position of poet laureate of England. Larkin revealed an intuitive awareness of "no-self" when he described the prospect of making his living as a poet: "If I'd tried in the forties and fifties, I'd have been a heap of whitened bones long ago. Nowadays you can live by being a poet. A lot of people do it: it means a blend of giving readings and lecturing and spending a year at a university as poet in residence or something.

But I couldn't bear that: it would embarrass me very much. I don't want to go around pretending to be me." He died in 1985.

Dorianne Laux was born in 1952 in Augusta, Maine. Laux worked a variety of jobs—as a cook in a sanatorium, a gas-station manager, and a maid—before receiving a BA in English from Mills College in 1988. Since then, she has taught creative writing at the University of Oregon, Pacific University, and North Carolina State University. She has also led summer workshops at the Esalen Institute in Big Sur, California. Her books include *What We Carry*, a finalist for the National Book Critics Circle Award; *Smoke*; *Facts about the Moon*, which won the Oregon Book Award; *The Book of Men*, which was awarded the Paterson Prize; and *Only as the Day Is Long: New and Selected*, which was a finalist for the Pulitzer Prize. She is the coauthor, with Kim Addonizio, of *The Poet's Companion: A Guide to the Pleasures of Writing Poetry*. Asked in an interview about whom she writes for, Laux replied, "Sometimes I write for or to a specific other, a beloved, other times for a small group of intimates, and sometimes I write to or for myself, some part of myself that asks to be questioned, confronted, consoled. . . . I do have a need to communicate, to commune, with others, whether distant or close, and so I'm always trying to connect, make some sense of things that don't cohere." Laux lives in Raleigh, North Carolina, with her husband, poet Joseph Millar.

Li-Young Lee was born in 1957 in Jakarta, Indonesia, to Chinese parents. His father had been a personal physician to Mao Zedong while in China, and moved the family to Indonesia, where he helped found Gamaliel University. In 1959, anti-Chinese sentiment forced the Lee family to flee Jakarta—Lee's father had been held as a political prisoner for a year—eventually settling in the United States in 1964. Lee studied at the University of Pittsburgh with Gerald Stern and has taught at Northwestern University and the University of Iowa. His books of poems include *The Undressing*, *Behind My Eyes*, *Book of My Nights*, and *The City in Which I Love You*. He has also published a memoir, *The Winged Seed: A Remembrance*, and a book of interviews, *Alabaster Jar: Conversations with Li-Young Lee*. Asked about the religious aspects of his work, Lee said "The whole enterprise of writing absolutely seems to me like a spiritual practice. It's a yoga. It's definitely part of my prayer life, my meditation life, my contemplative life. . . . You realize that the poem is a descendent of your psyche, but your psyche, if you pay attention, is a descendent of something else, let's say the cosmos. Then the cosmos is a descendent of something else, let's say the mind of God. So ultimately you go from the mind of God to the cosmos to the psyche to the poem. Those are concentric circles of embeddedness." Lee lives in Chicago.

Poet, critic, editor, and nonfiction writer **David Lehman** was born in 1948 in New York City, the son of European Holocaust refugees. He was educated at Columbia University and at Cambridge University in England. After various teaching stints, he left academia and made his living as a reviewer and freelance journalist for fifteen years, writing for such publications as *Newsweek*, the *Wall Street*

Journal, and the *New York Times*. A prolific editor and anthologist as well as poet and nonfiction writer, Lehman has been the series editor for *The Best American Poetry* yearly anthology since founding it in 1988. In 2006, he served as editor for the new *Oxford Book of American Poetry*. His other anthologies include *The Best American Erotic Poems* and *Great American Prose Poems*. His nonfiction work ranges from *One Hundred Autobiographies: A Memoir*, which recounts his struggle with cancer, to *Sinatra's Century*, and *A Fine Romance: Jewish Songwriters, American Songs*. His books of poetry include *The Daily Mirror*, *The Evening Sun*, *Poems in the Manner Of*, *The Morning Line*, and *New and Selected Poems*. Asked what advice he would give to young poets, Lehman said, "Make writing a habit you can't break, something you indulge in as regularly as coffee or tea. Read and absorb the great poems of the past; study them as needed; put in the time to get a grasp of the tradition, which is rich, and borrow or steal as needed." Lehman lives in New York City.

Denise Levertov was born in 1923 and grew up in Essex, England. At the age of twelve, she sent some of her poems to T. S. Eliot, who replied with a two-page letter of encouragement. During the Nazi Blitz of London, Levertov served as a civilian nurse. In 1948, she emigrated to America and soon moved beyond her early work in traditional forms, adopting an American idiom and a free verse largely influenced by William Carlos Williams. When the Vietnam War started, Levertov and several other writers founded the Writers and Artists Protest against the War in Vietnam. She participated in anti-war demonstrations and was jailed several times for civil disobedience. She was also a vocal opponent of nuclear weapons and environmental degradation. Her poems encompass both the political horrors of the twentieth century and the mystical dimensions of everyday life. "I saw Paradise," she wrote, "in the dust of the street." Her books include *Here and Now*, *O Taste and See!*, *A Door in the Hive*, and *The Great Unknowing: Last Poems*. She died in 1997.

Mexican-American poet **Ada Limón** was born in 1976 and grew up in Sonoma, California. She graduated with a degree in theater arts from the

University of Washington before earning an MFA in poetry from New York University in 2001. In 2022, she was appointed United States poet laureate. Her books include *Lucky Wreck*, *Bright Dead Things*, *The Hurting Kind*, and *The Carrying*, which won the National Book Critics Circle Award. In the *New York Times*, Ezra Klein observed that "Limón's poems are unique for the deep attention they pay to both the world's wounds and its redemptive beauty. In otherwise dark times, they have the power to open us up to the wonder and awe that the world still inspires." In an interview, Limón spoke about the relationship between poetry and grief, saying, "I think poetry is a way of carrying grief, but it's also a way of putting it somewhere so I don't always have to heave it onto my back or in my body. The more I put grief in a poem, the more I am able to move freely through the world, because I have named it, spoken it, and thrown it out into the sky." Limón lives in Lexington, Kentucky, and Sonoma, California.

Peggy Willis Lyles was born in Summerville, South Carolina, in 1939. After earning her BA from

Columbia College in South Carolina and an MA in English from Tulane University, she taught at Sophie Newcomb College and the University of Georgia. An influential editor as well as one of the most highly regarded haiku poets of her generation, Lyles was for many years a member of the *Red Moon Anthology* staff and editor at the *Heron's Nest*, a leading haiku journal. Her books include *Still at the Edge*, *Thirty-Six Tones*, and *To Hear the Rain: Selected Haiku of Peggy Lyles*. Asked in an interview where her inspiration for haiku came from, she said, "I think there is a nice paradox in haiku: the poet brings her whole life's experience, everything she is, to each one, and at the same time, virtually disappears into the details of the poem's moment. At best, haiku merge images from the exterior world with the landscape of the poet's heart so effectively that a receptive and fully participatory reader can become part of the poem, too." She died in 2010.

Born in 1920 in Cranston, Rhode Island, **Robert Major** grew up in Wickford, Rhode Island, and Columbus, Ohio, but has spent most of his adult life in the Pacific Northwest. He served in Europe during the Second World War as a member of the Ninth Air Corps, 404th Fighter Group. He went on to earn a degree in foreign service from Georgetown University and worked for the government in Washington, DC and in Montreal for several years. He was a professional editor for McGraw Hill in New York City before moving to Washington State and working at the University of Washington Office of Publications. While there, he earned a degree in fine arts. He also served for two years as the regional coordinator for the Northwest region of the Haiku Society of America. After the war, he became a Quaker and was an advocate for peace, playing an instrumental role in founding the Peace Park in Seattle. His books of haiku include *Shadows on the Soji*, *Sunlight Through Rain: A Northwest Haiku Year*, and *Coasting through Puddles: Haiku of Childhood*, which won the Virgil Hutton Haiku Memorial Award 2001–2. He died in 2008 in Bremerton, Washington.

Anne Haven McDonnell was born in 1968 and grew up in Boulder, Colorado. She is the author of *Breath on a Coal* and the chapbook *Living with Wolves*. Her honors include the Gingko Prize for Ecopoetry, a Terrain.org poetry prize, and a special mention for a 2021 Pushcart Prize. McDonnell received an MFA from the University of Alaska, Anchorage, and has been a writer-in-residence at the Andrews Forest Writing Residency, the Sitka Center for Art and Ecology, and the Wrangell Mountain Center in McCarthy, Alaska. She is a poetry editor at Terrain.org. In her personal statement upon receiving a National Endowment for the Arts grant, McDonnell said, "In a time of climate crisis and accelerating loss of species and unraveling ecosystems, I lean into poetry as a way to witness and speak towards this moment, towards grief and wonder in relationship with the living more-than-human world." McDonnell lives in Santa Fe, New Mexico, where she teaches as an associate professor at the Institute of American Indian Arts.

W. S. Merwin was born in New York City in 1927 and raised in New Jersey and Scranton, Pennsylvania. The son of a Presbyterian minister, Merwin began writing hymns as a child but would go on to find his own spiritual path in Buddhism and deep ecology. He graduated from Princeton in 1948 and spent an extra year studying Romance languages, a focus that would lead him to later become a prolific translator of poetry from Latin, Spanish, Japanese, and French. He won nearly every award available to an American poet and was twice named United States poet laureate. A staunch antiwar activist and environmentalist throughout his life, when Merwin won the Pulitzer Prize in 1970 for *The Carrier of Ladders*, he donated the one-thousand-dollar prize to antiwar causes in protest of the Vietnam War. In 1976, after Merwin moved to Hawaii to study with the Zen Buddhist master Robert Aitken, he created a nineteen-acre palm forest on what had been designated agricultural wasteland. Merwin's many books of poetry, prose, and translations include *The Lice*, *The Shadow of Sirius*, *The Vixen*, *Migration: New and Selected Poems*, *Collected Haiku of Yosa Buson*, and *Unframed Originals: Recollections*. As Peter Davison observed in the *Atlantic Monthly*, "The intentions of Merwin's poetry are as broad as the biosphere yet as intimate as a whisper.

He conveys in the sweet simplicity of grounded language a sense of the self where it belongs, floating between heaven, earth, and the underground." Merwin died in 2019.

Czesław Miłosz was born in 1911 in the village of Szetejnie, Lithuania. He wrote in Polish—he was also fluent in French, English, Lithuanian, and Russian—but considered himself to be both Polish and Lithuanian. "Language," he said, "is the only homeland." He endured World War II in Warsaw and was instrumental in helping Jews in Nazi-occupied Poland, for which he was awarded the medal of the Righteous Among Nations in Yad Vashem, Israel, in 1989. After the war, he served as Polish cultural attaché in Paris and defected to the West in 1951. His critical book *The Captive Mind* explores the dangers of totalitarianism and offers a searing critique of Soviet communism. From 1961 to 1998 he was a professor of Slavic languages and literatures at the University of California, Berkeley. Miłosz became a United States citizen in 1970 and, after the fall of the Iron Curtain, divided his time between Poland and the United States. He wrote in lonely obscurity for many years—the first book of his poetry to be translated into English did not appear until 1973. Because his books had been banned in Poland, many Polish readers were unaware of him until he was awarded the Nobel Prize in Literature in 1980. Discussing the intellectual repression he had witnessed, Miłosz said, "In a room where people unanimously maintain a conspiracy of silence, one word of truth sounds like a pistol shot." He died in 2004.

Lisel Mueller was born in Hamburg, Germany, in 1924. Both of her parents were teachers, and because of her father's outspoken criticism of the Nazis, the family was forced to flee Germany when Mueller was fifteen. They immigrated to the United States and settled outside of Chicago. Mueller graduated from the University of Evansville, where her father was a professor, and attended graduate school at Indiana University. Mueller taught at the University of Chicago, Goddard College, and Warren Wilson College. Her collections of poetry include

The Private Life, *The Need to Hold Still*, which received the National Book Award, and *Alive Together: New & Selected Poems*, which won the Pulitzer Prize. She has also published several books of translations, including *Circe's Mountain* by Marie Luise Kaschnitz. Describing her creative process in an interview, Mueller said, "Poems seem to strike me like lightning . . . and I never know where they come from and I never know when they come. It's always a matter of something connecting with something else, seeing something, hearing something that at another time would not have meant anything but, for some reason at that particular moment, . . . makes a new idea, a new way of seeing, a new perception." She died on February 21, 2020, at the age of ninety-six.

Carol Muske-Dukes was born in 1945 in St. Paul, Minnesota. She earned a BA from Creighton University and an MA from San Francisco State University. She has taught at the University of Southern California, where she founded the PhD program in creative writing and literature, as well as Columbia University, New York University, the Iowa Writers

Workshop, and the University of California at Irvine. She also founded a prison writing program at the New York Correctional Facility for Women on Rikers Island and later expanded the program to offer writing workshops in poetry, fiction, and playwriting throughout prisons in New York State. A former poet laureate of California (2008–11), her books of poetry include *Blue Rose*; *Twin Cities*; *Sparrow*, which was a National Book Award finalist; and *An Octave Above Thunder: New and Selected Poems*. In addition to poetry, she has published several novels, including *Channeling Mark Twain*, *Life After Death*, and *Saving St. Germ*, and a book of essays, *Married to an Ice-Pick Killer: A Poet in Hollywood*. She has won numerous awards for her work, including the Alice Fay Di Castagnola Award, an Ingram-Merrill Foundation grant, several Pushcart Prizes, and a Witter Bynner Fellowship Award from the Library of Congress. Asked about the role of poetry in our time, Muske-Dukes said, "The reality is that we live in an age that works against poetry. Poetry is an act of attention, and we're in a time where having an attention deficit is the norm. We're bombarded with images and information, but images and information are not knowledge—and they're certainly not poetry." Muske-Dukes lives in Los Angeles.

Pablo Neruda—dubbed "the greatest poet of the twentieth century in any language" by Colombian novelist Gabriel Garcia Márquez—was born Neftalí Ricardo Reyes Basoalto in 1904 in Parral, a wild region of central Chile. His father was a railway worker, and his mother, a schoolteacher, died when he was just two months old. Neruda began writing poems early and achieved worldwide fame when he published *Twenty Love Poems and a Song of Despair* when he was nineteen—a book for which he was paid five dollars. Neruda was hugely popular, once reading to a crowd of a hundred thousand people in São Paolo. He served as a diplomat in Ceylon, Burma, and Paris, and foreign dignitaries would often greet him by reciting one of his poems. As a member of the Chilean Communist Party, he was elected to the Senate in 1946. His furious denunciation of President Jorge Rafael Videla, who Neruda blamed for a massacre of coal miners, forced him to flee Chile in a daring escape on horseback over the Andes into Argentina. He ran for president in Chile, eventually stepping aside for his friend Salvador Allende. Neruda died on September 23, 1973, just days after the Pinochet-led coup that killed Allende. In 2013 Neruda's body was exhumed over suspicion that he might have been poisoned by the Pinochet regime. Evidence was inconclusive.

Born in the Bronx, New York, in 1932, **Linda Pastan** grew up in Westchester County, New York. Her father, a Jewish immigrant from Eastern Europe, was a surgeon. Her mother was a homemaker who sometimes helped with her husband's medical practice. Pastan graduated from Radcliffe College and then took a master's degree in library science from Simmons University in Boston, followed by an MA in English and American literature from Brandeis University. She is the author of fifteen books of poetry and essays, including *Almost an Elegy*, *Insomnia*, and *Carnival Evening: New and Selected Poems 1968–1998*, which was nominated for the National Book Award. Reflecting on her long career, Pastan said, "I think my poems have been consistent over the years in terms of their interest in metaphor, in the changing of the seasons, in Eden, in the dangers lurking beneath the surfaces of everyday life, in Death just waiting. And their ambition has always been to be both accessible on the surface and complex, even mysterious, underneath." Pastan served as the poet laureate of Maryland from 1991 to 1995, and was on the staff of the Bread Loaf Writers' Conference for twenty years. She died in 2023.

Lucia Perillo was born in 1958 and grew up in the suburbs of New York City. She graduated from McGill University in Montreal, where she studied wildlife management, and subsequently worked leading nature tours at the Denver Wildlife Research Center and at the San Francisco Bay Wildlife Refuge. She completed her MA in English at Syracuse University while working seasonally as a park ranger at Mount Rainier National Park. Her science background and intimate knowledge of plants and animals informs much of her poetry. She has also published a book of essays, *I Have Heard* *the Vultures Singing: Field Notes on Poetry, Illness, and Nature*, and a book of short stories, *Happiness Is a Chemical in the Brain*. In both her poetry and prose, she has written with extraordinary candor about living with multiple sclerosis. Her book *Spectrum of Possible Deaths* was a finalist for the 2012 National Book Award. Her most recent book is *Time Will Clean the Carcass Bones: Selected and New Poems*. She has taught at Syracuse University, Southern Illinois University, and in the MFA program at Warren Wilson College. A MacArthur Fellow, Perillo lived in Olympia, Washington, until her death in 2016.

Paulann Petersen was born in 1942 in Portland, Oregon, into a nonliterary, blue-collar family. She recalls that there wasn't a single book of poetry in her childhood home. Petersen attended Pomona College in California and was later a Wallace Stegner Fellow at Stanford University. She taught high school for many years in Klamath Falls and Portland, Oregon, and went on to become Oregon's sixth poet laureate. An ecstatic poet in the tradition of Whitman, Rumi, and Neruda, Petersen's books include *The Wild Awake*, *The Voluptuary*, *Understory*, and *My Kindred*. Of the beauty and variety of her home state, Petersen has written, "Oregon is mountains, ocean, high desert, rainforest. It's the hot springs in Hart Mountain Antelope Refuge, the Church of Elvis in downtown Portland, pelicans on Klamath Lake, herons in Oaks Bottom on the Willamette. Oregon is abundance, variety, vast and gorgeous. It teaches me inclusiveness and gratitude. Oregon encourages a wide embrace." Peterson lives in Portland, Oregon.

Justin Rigamonti was born in 1979 in Forest Grove, Oregon. He received an MFA in poetry at the University of California, Irvine, in 2009. Since then he has taught writing and poetry at Portland Community College, where he is the program coordinator for PCC's Carolyn Moore Writing Residency, the first and only program of its kind at a community college in the country. Rigamonti has published a picture book, *Pigs Went Marching Out!*, and collaborated on a children's board book, *My Little Blueberry*, with nationally acclaimed illustrator Beth Haidle. His poems have appeared in the *Threepenny Review*, *American Poetry Review*, *Smartish Pace*, *Thrush*, *New Ohio Review*, and elsewhere. He is also the editor of *The Great Uncluttering: The Collected Poetry of Carolyn Moore*. In an interview, Rigamonti said, "I think what draws me to poetry is the way that it expresses epiphany. Poetry goes for the moment, poetry tries to capture the moment of self-awareness, the moment of heartbreak, the moment of wonder." He lives in Portland, Oregon.

Rainer Maria Rilke was born in 1875, in Prague, then part of the Austro-Hungarian Empire. At age eleven, he began his formal schooling at a military boarding academy—his parents wanted him to become an officer, a position for which he was deeply unsuited—but was discharged in 1890 because of health problems that would affect him throughout his life. He went on to study literature, philosophy, and art history at Charles-Ferdinand University in Prague, and by 1896, had already published his first three volumes of poetry. In 1900, Rilke stayed at the artists' colony at Worpswede, Germany, where he met the sculptor Clara Westhoff, whom he married the following year. In 1902, he became the friend and, for a time, the secretary of Auguste Rodin. It was during his twelve-year Paris residence that Rilke enjoyed his greatest poetic activity. His first great work, *The Book of Hours*, appeared in 1905, followed by *New Poems* in 1907, and his only novel, *The Notebooks of Malte Laurids Brigge*, in 1910. When World War I broke out in 1914, Rilke was forced to leave France. He went first to Munich and then, in 1919, to Switzerland, where he spent the last years of his life. It was here that he wrote his last two great works, the *Duino Elegies* and the *Sonnets to Orpheus*, both in 1923. In his *Letters to a Young Poet*, Rilke said, "If your daily life seems poor, do not blame it; blame yourself, tell yourself that you are not poet enough to call forth its riches; for to the creator there is no poverty and no poor indifferent place." Rilke died of leukemia in 1926.

Valencia Robin was born in 1968 in Milwaukee, Wisconsin. An interdisciplinary artist whose practice includes poetry, painting, collage, and sculpture, she earned an MFA in art and design from the University of Michigan where she cofounded GalleryDAAS, an exhibition space that celebrates the creativity of artists of Africa and its diasporas. She also earned an MFA in creative writing from the University of Virginia. Robin's debut poetry collection, *Ridiculous Light*, won Persea Books' First Book Prize, was a finalist for the Kate Tufts Discovery Award, and was named one of *Library Journal*'s best poetry books of 2019. Robin offers readings, artist talks, class visits, and workshops at colleges and universities around the country. In an interview, she observed, "Poetry is a kind of spiritual practice for me; it allows me to deepen my experience of myself and the world." She currently teaches poetry at East Tennessee State University and lives in Johnson City, Tennessee.

Born in 1934 in Birmingham, Alabama, **Sonia Sanchez** experienced loss early in her life: her mother died when she was just a year old and her grandmother, when she was six. In 1943, she moved to Harlem to live with her father. She earned her BA in political science from Hunter College, followed by postgraduate work at New York University, where she studied poetry with Louise Bogan. Sanchez has written over a dozen books of poems, as well as short stories, critical essays, plays, and children's books. A leading member of the Black Arts Movement, Sanchez was instrumental in establishing the discipline of Black studies at university level. She was the first to teach a course based on Black women and literature in the United States, and the course she offered on African American literature at San Francisco State University is considered the first of its kind taught at a predominantly white school. Her many books include *Collected Poems*, *Shake Loose My Skin: New and Selected Poems*, *Homegirls and Handgrenades*, and *Morning Haiku*. In an interview, Sanchez reflected on discovering haiku, saying, "This poem, which was ancient, was also modern. . . . I realized it had already been written in my body, in my hand, in my head, before I wrote it down, that it was already in my breath, in my DNA. It was already in my bloodstream. I understood that through this form of seeking what I call 'another truth,' I was seeking the truth about what it meant to be Black, and the truth of my people, and my authority as a Black person and my right to be Black. But there's also the truth of beauty, and that's what I found." Sanchez was the first Presidential Fellow at Temple University where she taught from 1977 until her retirement in 1999. She lives in Philadelphia.

Born in 1923 in Chicago, **James Schuyler** grew up in Washington, DC, and East Aurora, New York. After serving as a sonar man on a destroyer during World War II, he attended Bethany College in West Virginia but did not graduate, claiming that he "spent more time playing bridge than studying." Schuyler worked for two years in Rome as a secretary for W. H. Auden. He then moved to New York City in 1950 and lived for a time with Frank O'Hara and John Ashbery. Like them, Schuyler was immersed in the art world; he wrote for *Art News* and became a curator of circulating exhibitions at the Museum of Modern Art. He also lived with the painter Fairfield Porter and his wife, the poet Anne Porter, for twelve years in East Hampton, New York. Schuyler's personal life was marked by financial stress and mental illness—he suffered a series of psychotic breaks and had to be repeatedly hospitalized—which made him increasingly reclusive in his later years. Unlike his fellow New York School poets, Schuyler was largely a pastoral poet, observing the changing weather and seasons with a scrupulous and tenderhearted attention—"the pure pleasure of simply looking"— reminiscent of ancient Chinese poetry. In his long poem, "Hymn to Life," Schuyler writes, "And there the Lincoln Memorial crumbles. It looks so solid: it won't / Last. The impermanence of permanence, is that all there is?" He won the Pulitzer Prize in 1980 for his book *The Morning of the Poem*. He died in 1991.

Heather Sellers was born in 1964 in Orlando, Florida. Her BA, MA, and PhD in creative writing are from Florida State University. She has taught writing at the University of Texas at San Antonio, Hope College, and St. Lawrence University, and is currently a professor of nonfiction and poetry at the University of South Florida in Tampa. Her books of poetry include *Drinking Girls and Their Dresses*; *The Boys I Borrow*, a James Laughlin Award finalist; *The Present*

State of the Garden; and *Field Notes from the Flood Zone*, which won a Florida Book Award. She is also the author of a memoir, *You Don't Look Like Anyone I Know*, about her experience with face blindness. The recipient of multiple teaching awards, she is the author of two textbooks, *The Practice of Creative Writing* and *How to Make Poems*. Reflecting on the spiritual dimensions of writing and teaching poetry, Sellers said, "Poetry is a reverence practice and an empathy practice, a way of paying attention to and holding close the world. In the classroom, a place where we practice together, we have a kind of sacred opportunity to transform our collective grief and joy into something truly sustaining." She lives in Tampa, Florida.

Edith Shiffert was born in Toronto in 1916. The family emigrated to the United States when Edith was three, and she grew up in upstate New York, Detroit, and Redondo Beach, California. She attended the University of Washington, where she concentrated on poetry and East Asian studies. There she studied with Theodore Roethke and served as co-editor of *Poetry Northwest*. In 1963, she moved to Kyoto, where she lived for more than fifty years, teaching at Doshisha University and Kyoto Seika College and becoming the most prominent American poet of her generation in that ancient seat of Japanese culture. The distinctive textures of daily life in Kyoto infuse her work, particularly her haiku, which she preferred to call simply "brief poems." She translated several volumes of Japanese poetry, including *Anthology of Modern Japanese Poetry* (with Yuki Sawa) and *Haiku Master Buson*, the first major translation into English of Buson's poetry and prose. Her many books include *Kyoto: The Forest Within the Gate*, *Kyoto Dwelling*, *Pathways*, *The Light Comes Slowly*, and *New and Selected Poems*. Kenneth Rexroth wrote that Shiffert's poetry "possesses an all-pervasive sweetness of temper, a graciousness that comes from a reverence for life and gratitude for being, her being and all being. Beyond her best poems is the echo of the bodhisattva vow and, at the same time, a realization that all the combinations called reality are fleeting by nature." Edith Shiffert died in Kyoto in 2017 at the age of 101.

William Stafford was born in 1914 in Hutchinson, Kansas. The family had to move frequently during the Great Depression for his father to find work, and Stafford helped out by delivering newspapers, working in the sugar-beet fields, and serving as an electrician's apprentice. Stafford's ethical principles showed early in his life when he defied segregation policies at the University of Kansas by sitting with African American students in the cafeteria. A Quaker and committed pacifist—one of "the quiet of the land"—he registered as a conscientious objector during World War II and worked in Civilian Public Service camps in Arkansas, California, and Illinois, which he wrote about in his memoir, *Down in My Heart*. His first book of poems, *West of Your City*, did not appear until he was forty-six. His second book, *Traveling Through the Dark*, won the National Book Award in 1963. Stafford claimed never to have suffered writer's block, insisting that if he ever felt he couldn't write, he simply lowered his standards. In his book on the writer's vocation, *Writing the Australian Crawl*, Stafford said, "A writer is not so much someone who has something to say as he is someone who has found a process that will bring about new things he would not have thought of if he hadn't started to say them." He died in 1993.

Ruth Stone was born in 1915 in Roanoke, Virginia, but lived most of her adult life in rural Vermont. She began writing poetry at the age of five and never stopped. She attended the University of Illinois at Urbana-Champaign and published her first book of poetry, *In an Iridescent Time*, in 1959. Soon after, her second husband, the poet and writer Walter Stone, committed suicide, leaving her to raise three young children alone. His death would haunt Stone's poetry for the rest of her life; she described her books as "love poems, all written to a dead man." She taught English and creative writing at Binghamton University for many years. Stone wrote in relative obscurity for much of her life but was greatly honored in her later years, winning the National Book Critics Circle Award for *Ordinary Life* in 1999 and the National Book Award for *In the Next Galaxy* in 2002. Her last book, *What Love Comes To: New and Selected Poems*, was a finalist for the Pulitzer Prize. A documentary film by Nora Jacobson, *Ruth Stone's Vast Library of the Female Mind*, was released in 2022. She died in 2011.

Latvian-Canadian poet, psychologist, and children's book writer, **George Swede** was born in 1940 in Riga, Latvia. When he was seven, Swede immigrated with his mother and stepfather to Oyama, British Columbia, eventually moving to Vancouver. He graduated with a BA in psychology from the University of British Columbia and an MA in psychology from Dalhousie University. He taught psychology for many years at Ryerson University (now Toronto Metropolitan University). Among his many books of poetry are *The Way a Poem Emerges: A Haiku Trinity and Beyond*, *helices*, *Almost Unseen: Selected Haiku of George Swede*, and *Global Haiku*. On the immediacy of haiku, Swede once said, "I have always nurtured a connection with the immediately perceived: in a forest, or in the center of a large city, or in my study. It seems to give me the grounding necessary to not be overwhelmed by the suffering that surrounds us in its many guises." He lives in Toronto, Canada.

Arthur Sze was born in the Bronx, New York, in 1950 to Chinese immigrant parents. He grew up in New York City and Garden City, New Jersey, though he has spent most of his adult life in New Mexico, whose culture and landscape are strongly present in his poetry. He has taught extensively in the New Mexico Poets-in-the-Schools program, as well as at the Institute of American Indian Arts. Sze has translated ancient Chinese poetry, and his early work especially shows the influences of the major Tang dynasty poets Wang Wei, Li Bai, and Du Fu. In an interview, Sze spoke about what moves him to write poetry: "I love the intensity and power of language, emotion, and imagination that all come together in poetry. It's an essential language and as necessary as breathing. It helps me live and grow in the world. . . . Solitary as this practice is, I hope that my poetry, like all poetry, speaks to others and is a gift that awakens and moves others to experience the world in profound, essential ways." Sze's books include *The Glass Constellation: New and Collected Poems*; *Sight Lines*, which won the 2019 National Book Award; *Compass Rose*; and *The Ginkgo Light*. He has also published *The Silk Dragon: Translations from the Chinese*. A professor emeritus at the Institute of American Indian Arts, Sze lives in Santa Fe.

Nobel Laureate **Wisława Szymborska** was born in 1923 in Prowent, Poland, but her family moved to Warsaw when she was eight, and she spent the rest of her life there. She began writing poetry at the age of four. Like Czesław Miłosz and many other Polish writers, she witnessed the horrors of World War II and endured the brutality of the Soviet occupation, both of which profoundly influenced her poetry. After the war, she studied Polish literature and sociology at Jagiellonian University and worked as an editor and columnist. Though she became a member of the Polish Communist Party in 1952 and supported socialist themes in her early work, even writing a poem to Lenin, she later disavowed her first two books of political poetry. Her mature work frequently undermines collectivist abstractions and grand political themes in favor of the individual and the ordinary/extraordinary objects and events of daily life in poems that are both playful and philosophical, transparent and profoundly complex. Szymborska became hugely popular in Poland. Polish rock singer Kora turned her poem "Nothing Twice" into a hit song, and her poem "Love at First Sight" inspired the enigmatic film *Red* by the Polish director Krzysztof Kieslowski. In awarding her the Nobel Prize in Literature in 1996, the committee called Szymborska a "Mozart of poetry." She died in 2012.

Natasha Trethewey was born in Gulfport, Mississippi, in 1966. Her parents were forced to travel to Ohio to marry, as interracial marriage was still illegal in Mississippi. Trethewey's birth certificate listed the race of her mother as "colored" and the race of her father as "Canadian." Her mother, Gwendolyn Ann Turnbough, was a social worker and part of the inspiration for *Native Guard*, which is dedicated to her. Trethewey's parents divorced when she was six; twelve years later her mother was murdered by her second husband, whom she had recently divorced. Trethewey said "that was the moment when I both felt that I would become a poet and then immediately afterward felt that I would not. I turned to poetry to make sense of what had happened." She has recently also published *Memorial Drive: A Daughter's Memoir* to fully tell the story of her mother's life and death. In an interview, Trethewey said, "I think that I have two existential wounds that make me a writer, and one of them is that great loss. I think that's my deepest wound, losing my mother, but the other one is the wound of history that has everything to do with being born Black and biracial in a place that would render me illegitimate in the eyes of the law, a place that has tried to remind Black people for centuries of our second-class status, with Confederate monuments, with the Confederate flag, with Jim Crow laws, with all sorts of things that are part of our shared history as Americans." Trethewey's books of poetry include *Beyond Katrina*; *Thrall*; *Native Guard*, which was awarded the 2007 Pulitzer Prize; and *Monument: Poems New and Selected*. She served two terms as United States poet laureate from 2012 to 2014. She lives in Evanston, Illinois.

Vincent Tripi was born Vincent Garzilli in Brooklyn, New York, in 1941 and assumed his mother's maiden name when he started writing haiku in the 1980s. He is most closely associated with the spiritual movement in American haiku. His studies in philosophy and later psychology led to a career in children's services, crisis intervention, and especially residential treatment. He also taught yoga and meditation for many years. In the early '80s he moved to a cabin in New Hampshire and assumed a solitary life that led to his first book, *Haiku Pond: A Track of the Trail and Thoreau*. His other books of haiku include *Paperweight for Nothing*, *Path of a Bird*, *Between God & the Pine*, and *Somewhere Among the Clouds: Poems from a Year in Solitude*. After moving to San Francisco in 1989, he helped form the Haiku Poets of Northern California and was instrumental in creating their first magazine, *Woodnote*, which he co-edited with the late haiku master Paul O. Williams. In 2006 he founded the Haiku Circle, a unique gathering of haiku poets which takes place each year in Athol, Massachusetts. He lived the last twenty years of his life in western Massachusetts. Tripi died in 2020.

William Carlos Williams was born in 1883 in Rutherford, New Jersey, and lived his whole life there, apart from his years at the University of Pennsylvania, where he studied medicine and was friends with Ezra Pound. He became a family doctor, tending primarily to poor Italian and Polish immigrants, making house calls, calming fevers, and delivering babies at all hours, often without pay. He was a central figure in the modernist revolution and sought to strip language clean of its encrusted poetic associations and to speak in a distinctively American idiom. Williams rejected what he saw as the disillusionment and cultural elitism of T. S. Eliot and tried to bring poetry closer to lived experience. "No ideas but in things," he wrote, and many of his poems have the hard, clear, "just-this" quality of Zen. Though he had to pay for the publication of his first four books of poems, he went on to win both the National Book Award and the Pulitzer Prize, and was recognized as one of the great poets of the twentieth century. He died in 1963.

Haiku poet **John Wills** was born in 1921 in Los Angeles, California. He received an MA from the

University of Chicago in 1951, and a PhD from Washington University in St. Louis in 1961. For more than two decades, he taught American and English literature at universities in Ohio, Wisconsin, Minnesota, North Dakota, North Carolina, Georgia, and Tennessee, and during that time, he published critical essays on T. S. Eliot, Joseph Conrad, and other writers. After the death of his first wife, he married artist and poet Marlene Morelock (later known as Marlene Mountain). They worked together on several haiku projects that incorporated her drawings and photographs with Wills's haiku. In 1970, Wills spent the summer studying haiku in Matsuyama, Japan, under a research grant from Georgia Southern College. In 1971, he moved with his family to Tennessee, where they lived in the mountains on one hundred acres of land, which they named "Sweetwater" and where much of his best work was written. Speaking about the haiku tradition in an interview, Wills said, "We have [learned] and still do learn from the Japanese, of course, and from Western literature, too. But we must after that write our own poetry; there's no other way." His many books include *Weathervanes*, *Back Country*, *Cornstubble*, and *Up a Distant Ridge*. He died in 1993.

James Wright was born in 1927 in Martins Ferry, Ohio, to working-class parents, neither of whom attended school beyond the eighth grade. His early life was marked by poverty and a nervous breakdown that would force him to miss a year of high school. He served in the army in Japan during the American occupation and then attended Kenyon College, where he studied with John Crowe Ransom and later with Theodore Roethke and Stanley Kunitz at the University of Washington. Wright suffered depression and bipolar disorder, and struggled with alcoholism. He had to be hospitalized on several occasions and was subjected to electroshock therapy. With his friend Robert Bly, he translated German and South American poets and was deeply influenced by ancient Chinese and Japanese poetry, influences he brought to bear with brilliant effect on poems about the postindustrial American Midwest. His books include *The Branch Will Not Break*, *Shall We Gather at the River*, *Saint Judas*, and *This Journey*. Karen

Whitehall in the *Virginia Quarterly Review* observed that what makes Wright a great poet is "his constant openheartedness: he is not self-absorbed. His work explores a full range of feeling; he found much to celebrate and praise as well as to lament; he affirmed the good in life however limited." Wright won the Pulitzer Prize in 1972 for his *Collected Poems*. He died in 1980.

Alan Yan was born in Pittsburgh, Pennsylvania, in 1994, the son of Chinese parents who emigrated from Shanghai in the late 1980s. He studied product design at Duke University and the Massachusetts Institute of Technology. Yan's poems have appeared in the *Westchester Review* and the *Bangalore Review*, and his haiku have been published in *Modern Haiku* and *Presence*. He lives in Brooklyn, New York.

One of Ireland's greatest poets, **William Butler Yeats** was born in Dublin in 1865 and educated there and in London. He spent childhood holidays in County Sligo and was influenced by both the landscape and the folklore of that place. Yeats was deeply involved in politics and served as an Irish senator for two terms. He also had a lifelong interest in mystical pursuits, including spiritualism, Theosophy, séances, astrology, hermeticism, automatic writing, and the occult. He was a seeker of ultimate truths—"Talent perceives differences," he wrote, "genius, unity"—and in his book *A Vision* he developed a mystical system to explain his theories of physical and spiritual masks and the cycles of life. In 1923 he was awarded the Nobel Prize in Literature for what the Nobel committee described as "inspired poetry, which in a highly artistic form gives expression to the spirit of a whole nation." Yeats famously likened the poetic process to a lover's quarrel with oneself: "We make out of the quarrel with others, rhetoric, but of the quarrel with ourselves, poetry." He died in 1939.

Kevin Young was born in 1970, in Lincoln, Nebraska, and grew up primarily in Topeka, Kansas. Young graduated from Harvard University in 1992, where he studied with Seamus Heaney and Lucie Brock-Broido. While at Harvard, he became a member of the Dark Room Collective, a community of African American writers in Boston that included Major Jackson, Natasha Trethewey, Elizabeth Alexander, and many others. After a Wallace Stegner Fellowship at Stanford University, where he worked with Denise Levertov, Young received his MFA from Brown University. He is currently the Andrew W. Mellon Director of the Smithsonian's National Museum of African American History and Culture and the poetry editor of the *New Yorker*. Young has published many books of poetry, including *Stones, Books of Hours,* and *Blue Laws: Selected & Uncollected Poems 1995–2015*. He is also the editor of several acclaimed anthologies, including *The Art of Losing: Poems of Grief & Healing*, *Jazz Poems*, and *African-American Poetry: 250 Years of Struggle & Song*. In an interview, Young said, "A poem can provide testimony, a poem can provide solace, it can provide a connection. But it also can provide a sense of something you knew was there but you couldn't quite put into words: I think they can often articulate for you—and this is as true for the poet as it is for the reader—something you didn't quite know. That sense of mystery, but also of revelation, is what I turn to poems for." Young lives in New York City.

Adam Zagajewski was born in 1945 in Lvov, Poland, but the family was expelled to central Poland in 1946. He lived in Berlin for several years, moved to France in 1982, and has taught at universities in the United States, including the University of Houston and the University of Chicago. Considered one of the "Generation of '68" or "New Wave" writers in Poland, Zagajewski wrote protest poetry early in his career, though his later work is more lyrical. The poet and critic Robert Pinsky wrote that Zagajewski's poems are "about the presence of the past in ordinary life: history not as chronicle of the dead, or an anima to be illuminated by some doctrine, but as an immense, sometimes subtle force inhering in what people see and feel every day—and in the ways we see and feel." His books of poetry include *Without End: New and Selected Poems*, *Asymmetry*, *True Life*, and *Mysticism for Beginners*. He also published two books of essays, *A Defense of Ardor* and *Slight Exaggeration*. Zagajewski died in 2021.

Credits

Diligent efforts were made in every case to identify copyright holders of the poems. The author and the publisher are grateful for the use of this material.

Elizabeth Alexander, "Praise Song for the Day" and "Autumn Passage" from *Crave Radiance: New and Selected Poems 1990–2010*. Copyright © 2008 by Elizabeth Alexander. Reprinted with the permission of The Permissions Company, LLC, on behalf of Graywolf Press, graywolfpress.org and the Faith Childs Literary Agency.

A. R. Ammons, "Poetics" and "Still" from *The Complete Poems of A. R. Ammons, Volume 1 1955–1966*. Copyright © 1965 by A. R. Ammons. Used by permission of W. W. Norton & Company, Inc.

Ellen Bass, "Ode to Fat" from *Indigo*. Copyright © 2020 by Ellen Bass. Reprinted with the permission

Acknowledgments

I'm profoundly grateful to Heather Sellers for helping me with every aspect of this anthology. Her contributions, from the book's inception to its completion, have been so essential she rightly should be credited as co-editor. I'm thankful to my wife, Alice Boyd, for her unerring ability to confirm (and sometimes disconfirm) my choices. Andrea Hollander, Justin Rigamonti, and Alan Yan also provided helpful comments and suggestions. Laura Cunningham once again brought her sharp eye and light touch to the editing of the manuscript, encouraging me to make it stronger when I thought I was done. I'm grateful as well to Daniel Aitken, Kat Davis, Patty McKenna, Ben Gleason, and the whole team at Wisdom Publications for believing in this book and making me feel again a part of the Wisdom family. A deep bow to you all.

A slightly different version of "The Art of Appreciative Attention" appeared in *Watkins Mind Body Spirit*.

About the Editor

John Brehm was born and raised in Lincoln, Nebraska, and educated at the University of Nebraska and Cornell University. He is the author of four books of poetry—*Sea of Faith, Help Is on the Way, No Day at the Beach,* and *Dharma Talk*—as well as a collection of essays, *The Dharma of Poetry.* He is the editor of the best-selling anthology *The Poetry of Impermanence, Mindfulness, and Joy.* His poems have appeared in *Poetry, Ploughshares, The Gettysburg Review, The Sun, The Southern Review, Plume, The Writer's Almanac, Poetry Daily, Verse Daily, The Best American Poetry,* and many other journals and anthologies. With his wife, Feldenkrais teacher Alice Boyd, he leads retreats that incorporate

Feldenkrais Awareness Through Movement Lessons, meditation, and mindful poetry discussions. johnbrehmpoet.com.

What to Read Next from Wisdom Publications

Poetry of Impermanence, Mindfulness, and Joy
John Brehm

"This collection would make a lovely gift for a poetry-loving or dharma-practicing friend, it could also serve as a wonderful gateway to either topic for the uninitiated." —*Tricycle: The Buddhist Review*

Dharma Talk
Poems
John Brehm

"Think of this collection as a Guidebook to Emptiness—to everything and nothing (which, as the poet tells us, are interchangeable). Brehm gives us a taste of that everything in images ranging from jasmine blossoms placed beside the bed to perfume the dreamer's sleep, to a brain bathed in sea salt and lavender. These collected lines hang in the air like the spider's web described in Brehm's poem 'Design':

'knowing / just how / much to give / in either / direc-
tion / without breaking.' *Dharma Talk* is full of won-
ders." —Danusha Laméris, author of *Bonfire Opera*

The Dharma of Poetry
How Poems Can Deepen Your Spiritual Practice and Open You to Joy
John Brehm

"*The Dharma of Poetry* is a warm invitation to explore the
beauty of our own lives, retrieving a sense of wonder
and mystery as we navigate both the immediate and
the timeless. John Brehm has done a masterful job in
reminding us of the power of our own poetic sensi-
bilities." —Joseph Goldstein, author of *The Experience of
Insight*, *A Heart Full of Peace*, and *Mindfulness: A Practical Guide
to Awakening*

Bearing the Unbearable
Love, Loss, and the Heartbreaking Path of Grief
Joanne Cacciatore

"Simultaneously heartwrenching and uplifting.
Cacciatore offers practical guidance on coping with
profound and life-changing grief. This book is des-
tined to be a classic . . . simply the best book I have
ever read on the process of grief." —Ira Israel, *The
Huffington Post*

Grieving Is Loving
Compassionate Words for Bearing the Unbearable
Joanne Cacciatore

"*Grieving Is Loving* is a wise, moving, and compassionate book. Reading it brought tears to my eyes as it reminded me of the loss of loved ones thirty and forty-five years ago. Not only should its message be read and internalized by those suffering the loss of a beloved, but also by those with friends who have lost or are likely to lose someone in the future—in other words, by everyone." —Irving Kirsch, PhD, Harvard Medical School, University of Connecticut, University of Hull, author of *The Emperor's New Drugs: Exploding the Antidepressant Myth*

Zen Encounters with Loneliness
Terrance Keenan

"Every few years, if you're lucky, a book comes along that changes your life. *Zen Encounters with Loneliness* is one of those books." —Satya Robyn, author of *Afterwards*

About Wisdom Publications

Wisdom Publications is the leading publisher of classic and contemporary Buddhist books and practical works on mindfulness. To learn more about us or to explore our other books, please visit our website at wisdomexperience. org or contact us at the address below.

Wisdom Publications
132 Perry Street
New York, NY 10014 USA

We are a 501(c)(3) organization, and donations in support of our mission are tax deductible.

Wisdom Publications is affiliated with the Foundation for the Preservation of the Mahayana Tradition (FPMT).